THE TRUTH ABOUT VIOLENCE

MARK J. KITTLESON, PH.D.
Southern Illinois University
General Editor

WILLIAM KANE, PH.D.
University of New Mexico
Adviser

RICHELLE RENNEGARBE, PH.D.
McKendree College
Adviser

Karl Larson
Principal Author

William McCay
Contributing Author

☑®
Facts On File, Inc.

The Truth About Violence

Facts On File, Inc.
132 West 31st Street
New York NY 10001

Library of Congress Cataloging-in-Publication Data

The truth about violence / Mark J. Kittleson, general editor; William Kane, adviser; Richelle Rennegarbe, adviser; Karl Larson and William McCay, authors.
   p. cm.
   Includes index
   ISBN 0-8160-5302-2 (hc: alk. paper)
   1. Violence in adolescence–United States–Juvenile literature. 2. Teenagers–United States–Juvenile literature. I. McCay, William. II. Kittleson, Mark J., 1952– III. Title.
   HQ799.2.V56L37 2005
   303.6'0973–dc22   2004030218

Facts On File books are available at special discounts when purchased in bulk quantities for businesses, associations, institutions, or sales promotions. Please call our Special Sales Department in New York at (212) 967-8800 or (800) 322-8755.

You can find Facts On File on the World Wide Web at http://www.factsonfile.com

Text design by David Strelecky
Cover design by Cathy Rincon
Graphs by Jeremy Eagle

Printed in the United States of America

MP Hermitage 10 9 8 7 6 5 4 3 2 1

This book is printed on acid-free paper.

CONTENTS

LIST OF ILLUSTRATIONS AND TABLES

PREFACE

In developing The Truth About series, we have taken time to review some of the most pressing problems facing our youths today. Issues such as alcohol and drug abuse, depression, family problems, sexual activity, and eating disorders are at the top of a list of growing concerns. It is the intent of these books to provide vital facts while also dispelling myths about these terribly important and all-too-common situations. These are authoritative resources that kids can turn to in order to get an accurate answer to a specific question or to research the history of a problem, giving them access to the most current related data available. It is also a reference for parents, teachers, counselors, and others who work with youths and require detailed information.

Let's take a brief look at the issues associated with each of those topics. Alcohol and drug use and abuse continue to be a national concern. Today's young people often use drugs to avoid the extraordinary pressures of today. In doing so they are losing their ability to learn how to cope effectively. Without the internal resources to cope with pressure, adolescents turn increasingly back to addictive behaviors. As a result, the problems and solutions are interrelated. Also, the speed with which the family structure is changing often leaves kids with no outlet for stress and no access to support mechanisms.

In addition, a world of youths faces the toughest years of their lives, dealing with the strong physiological urges that accompany sexual desire. Only when young people are presented the facts honestly, without indoctrination, are they likely to connect risk taking with certain behaviors. This reference set relies on knowledge as the most important tool in research and education.

Finally, one of the most puzzling issues of our times is that of eating disorders. Paradoxically, while our youths are obsessed with thinness and beauty and go to extremes to try to meet perceived societal expectations, they are also increasingly plagued by obesity. Here, too, separating the facts from fiction is an important tool in research and learning.

As much as possible, The Truth About presents the facts through honest discussions and reports of the most up-to-date research. Knowing the facts associated with health-related questions and problems will help young people make informed decisions in school and throughout life.

Mark J. Kittleson
General Editor

HOW TO USE THIS BOOK

NOTE TO STUDENTS

Knowledge is power. By possessing knowledge you have the ability to make decisions, ask follow-up questions, or know where to go to obtain more information. In the world of health that *is* power! That is the purpose of this book—to provide you with the power you need to obtain unbiased, accurate information and *The Truth About Violence.*

Topics in each volume of The Truth About series are arranged in alphabetical order, from A to Z. Each of these entries defines its topic and explains in detail the particular issue. At the end of most entries are cross-references to related topics. A list of all topics by letter can be found in the table of contents or at the back of the book in the index.

How have these books been compiled? First, the publisher worked with me to identify some of the country's leading authorities on key issues in health education. These individuals were asked to identify some of the major concerns that young people have about such topics. The writers read the literature, spoke with health experts, and incorporated their own life and professional experiences to pull together the most up-to-date information on health issues, particularly those of interest to adolescents and of concern in Healthy People 2010.

Throughout the alphabetical entries, the reader will find sidebars that separate Fact from Fiction. There are Question-and-Answer boxes that attempt to address the most common questions that youths ask about sensitive topics. In addition, readers will find a special feature called "Teens Speak"—case studies of teens with personal stories related to the topic in hand.

This may be one of the most important books you will ever read. Please share it with your friends, families, teachers, and classmates. Remember, you possess the power to control your future. One way to affect your course is through the acquisition of knowledge. Good luck and keep healthy.

NOTE TO LIBRARIANS

This book, along with the rest of The Truth About series, serves as a wonderful resource for young researchers. It contains a variety of facts, case studies, and further readings that the reader can use to help answer questions, formulate new questions, or determine where to go to find more information. Even though the topics may be considered delicate by some, do not be afraid to ask patrons if they have questions. Feel free to direct them to the appropriate sources, but do not press them if you encounter reluctance. The best we can do as educators is to let young people know that we are there when they need us.

Mark J. Kittleson, Ph.D.
General Editor

VIOLENT BEHAVIOR AND PERSONAL SAFETY

Violence is the use of force, either in action or behavior, to harm another person. For most people, the word *violence* suggests physical harm, but violence can also result in emotional or mental distress. The concept of violence covers a broad range of behavior. It includes shootings, robbery, sexual assault or rape, child abuse, spousal abuse, and any other form of physical assault on another person. Throughout this book such acts fall under the category of violent crime. There is also the violence that is an integral part of war. And increasingly Americans are experiencing terrorism. A form of violence directed at civilians and political leaders, terrorism is meant to instill fear and to force political change, allowing a small number of people to have a devastating impact on a whole society. However, there are less obvious forms of violence.

Bullying may or may not include physical harm. Creating fear in a classmate is a form of bullying, although the aggressive student may never physically touch his or her victim. Neglect is a form of violence in which *not* doing something is the crime. Manipulating the feelings of children and intimate partners is a form of violence commonly called emotional abuse. In fact, this type of abuse can create such a fearful environment that daily living becomes a challenge. This book will discuss many forms of violent behavior, their origins, and how they impact individuals and communities.

It seems almost impossible to escape violence these days. Turn on the television news, read a newspaper, or even talk to your friends in the lunchroom, and you'll hear about some sort of violence. Thousands get killed every day in our nation, and many times more suffer injury, humiliation, embarrassment, threats, violation, robbery, or torture. Americans are confronted with so much violence today that many people react to stories about violent acts with a shrug, perhaps suggesting violence seems beyond anyone's control.

A HISTORY OF VIOLENCE

Violence has impacted humanity since before history. Even the earliest human cultures killed in order to eat meat and wear animal skins. Studying the fossil record of North and South America, paleoarcheologists, scientists who examine the remains of prehistoric cultures, found a remarkably efficient spearhead called the Clovis point that was made in North America approximately 15,000 years ago. As scientists tracked the spread of the Clovis point, they noticed that the remains of large mammals like the mammoth and the giant sloth decreased. The animals became extinct—hunted out of existence by people who killed them for sustenance.

As civilization developed, violence did not disappear. For more than 600 years, citizens of Rome filled large arenas to watch gladiators fight to the death. In the 1600s the English theater that produced William Shakespeare's plays was located near a bear-garden. Here, bears would be chained to a post to fight to the death with pairs of dogs. Fans included King Henry VIII and Queen Elizabeth I.

Today the words *prize fight* evoke the image of a boxing match. However, the term developed from the prizes given in professional swordfights in which participants faced injury and even death. British newspaper reports from the 1700s describe fights that were scored by how many wounds each competitor gave and received. During those years, the weapons changed from swords to clubs and staffs, and finally to fists.

The spectacle of violent death continued to draw the public, as revealed by the large numbers of people who gathered to witness public executions. In the United States, as recently as 1934, a crowd of 20,000 gathered for the last execution that allowed unrestricted public participation.

People no longer watch public executions, but they bring violence into their homes through blood-spattered TV shows and videos. They also participate in simulated beatings, shootings, and bloodshedding in ever-more-realistic video games.

For years, researchers have tried to figure out why some people become violent. Everyone deals with conflict day in and day out, yet very few people commit acts of violence. What influences some individuals to respond to conflicts or problems with violence?

Some researchers believe that people are born with a predisposition toward violence. Still others believe the roots of violence lie in a person's upbringing and environment. The answer may be found in a combination or the interaction of these factors. To date, scientists have enjoyed more success in classifying violence than understanding its causes.

COMMON ACTS OF VIOLENCE

As part of a program to provide a uniform annual report of crimes in the United States, the Federal Bureau of Investigation (FBI) has developed general definitions of many forms of violence. Violent crimes include four offenses:

- Homicide consists of murder and nonnegligent manslaughter, defined as the intentional killing of one human being by another. Suicide is not included in this offense. Attempts to murder are classified as aggravated assaults.
- Rape, or forcible rape, defined as sexual intercourse with a female forcibly and against her will. Attempts to commit rape by force or threat of force are also included.
- Robbery, defined as taking or attempting to take anything of value from the care or control of a person by force or threat of force or violence and/or by putting the victim in fear.
- Assault, or aggravated assault, defined as an unlawful attack by one person upon another for the purpose of inflicting bodily injury, usually involving a weapon. Incidents of displaying or threatening with a gun, knife, or other weapon which could cause bodily harm are included.

Property crimes include the offenses of burglary, larceny/theft, motor vehicle theft, and arson. The offenses involve the taking of money or property, or destroying it. These crimes violate a person's sense of safety and create fear, but they are not classified as violent by the FBI.

Other forms of violence which may involve law enforcement agencies include simple assault. This occurs when someone attacks, menaces, or intimidates another person without the use of a weapon. Police may also intervene in cases of domestic violence. Also known as family violence, this category includes cases of simple assault that take place in a home environment. Such cases also include spousal or intimate partner abuse, parental or elder abuse, and sibling abuse.

WHAT FACTORS CONTRIBUTE TO VIOLENCE?

National and international agencies increasingly view the problem of violence as a public health issue. The World Health Organization, the global public health body of the United Nations, has issued a report on the worldwide implications of violence. In the United States, the surgeon general, the nation's highest-ranking public health officer, has issued several reports on violence, especially among young people. Agencies like the Centers for Disease Control and Prevention (CDC), the National Institute on Drug Abuse, and the National Institute on Alcohol Abuse and Alcoholism have all worked on violence-related research, as has the Department of Health and Human Services. This research has resulted in identifying a number of symptoms of violence but few cures.

Violence and victims

In 2000, the U.S. Department of Justice estimated that some 7 million violent crimes occur in the United States annually and each one had at least one victim.

How do so many people end up as victims of a crime? There are many possible reasons. At times people take risks that put them in danger. For instance, if a person works at night and walks to his or her car alone in the dark, he or she may risk a robbery or an assault. The odds go up considerably if the person is a female. Some people feel a sense of security because nothing has ever happened to them or to anyone they know. Nonetheless, they are still at risk. In many cases, criminals watch their victims for some time before they act.

According to statistics from the Department of Justice, one in every five violent crimes happens on a street away from one's home, and one in every seven violent crimes occurs in a parking lot or commercial building. One in every three armed robberies or assaults takes place at night, between 6 P.M. and midnight.

Walking alone at night is only one example of risky behavior. The use of alcohol and drugs also increases one's risk of becoming a victim. Drugs and alcohol can also affect one's judgment on a date. Being intoxicated makes one more vulnerable to rape or robbery. Research shows that people arrested for drug dealing often become involved in this dangerous trade while trying to make enough money to support their own drug habits. Their addiction has forced them into serious and even violent business to pay for it.

These examples serve to reinforce the old saying "Look before you leap." The excitement of the moment may lead people to try things they would not normally do. This happens to everyone at some point in time, and most are lucky enough not to end up in danger because of unwise choices. But the risks are real, and a little planning can save a lot of headaches and heartaches down the road.

On occasion, people find themselves in the wrong place at the wrong time. Large-scale violence usually takes its victims by surprise. Take, for example, the bombing at the Olympic Park during the 1996 Summer Games in Atlanta. Two people were killed in that blast, and another 111 were injured. All count as victims of violence. All were simply in the wrong place at the wrong time. Other examples include the bombing of Oklahoma City's Alfred P. Murrah Federal Building in May 1995 and the destruction of the World Trade Center towers on September 11, 2001. Thousands of innocent victims died in those attacks.

Characteristics of victims

For young people, there is no question that violence is a very real problem. Whatever the type of violent crime, the patterns of victimization indicate that teens are the group hardest hit. According to government statistics, the involvement of young people in violent crimes rises until age 21 and only then begins to fall. In 2003, one of three murder victims and one in two assault victims in the United States was under 25. One in five of all rape victims was under the age of 21. Teens were victims of half of all robberies. Young Americans make up the majority of all victims of violence.

On average, one of every four high school students has experienced dating violence. Adolescent girls are the more likely victims. Dating violence may involve physical violence, such as striking one's date or forcing sexual activity, but it also includes verbal threats, intimidation, or emotional abuse.

Bullying represents another form of violence often specific to young people. Sometimes the victims accept abuse passively or sub-missively, sending out the message that they are weak or insecure and that they will probably not fight back if picked on. They may not be weak at all, but their fear sends signals to aggressive schoolmates looking for a target. They might not be as talented or athletic as their peers, or they might be shy and are perceived as weak. Others are called provocative victims. The provocative victim can be anxious or aggressive, generally hot-tempered, and might even pick fights but usually loses them.

When violence occurs in the home between members of the same family, it is called domestic or family violence. Victims of family vio-lence are usually women and children. Men are most often the aggressors in family violence rather than the victims. Victims may not only be physically harmed but also emotionally damaged through constant insults, threats, or humiliation. Women who are victims of family violence often feel as though they cannot leave the relation-ship because of children, financial security, or fears for their safety.

Hate crimes are acts of violence inflicted on individuals because of their race, ethnicity, gender, or sexual orientation. The most common acts of violence involve hitting, kicking, verbal harassment, or threats. One in seven hate crime victims also has their personal prop-erty vandalized with symbols or slogans of an offensive nature.

Violence and perpetrators

Just as no standard description of a victim exists, no standard description of a violent person exists. In 1999, law enforcement agen-cies made 635,000 arrests for violent offenses in the United States. More than 100,000 of those arrested were children under the age of 18. Criminal offenders had many different motivations and became violent for a wide variety reasons.

Some scientists theorize that a tendency toward violence may be hereditary, but there is little evidence to support that theory. Most social scientists believe that violence is a learned behavior. People learn how to be violent through what they see in their home and their community. Researchers have spent decades collecting evidence to indicate that young people who watch violence on television are more likely to act in a violent fashion than those who do not. Violent tel-evision programs and movies tend to desensitize viewers, who are then less likely to consider the consequences of a violent act or to be shocked by an act of violence.

Psychological studies also support the theory that people who grow up seeing violence perpetrated by adults or who are abused as children are more likely to accept violence as an appropriate means of dealing with conflict as adults.

People who display violent behavior are often deficient in social skills. Rather than using communication to avoid a confrontation or defuse a conflict, they see an act of violence as the first and best solution. Think of the last time a fight happened in your school. Did the people involved make an attempt to discuss the conflict? Did either person clarify what the fight was about? Did anyone try to reach a mutual agreement or find compromise on the issue? Probably not. Fighters see conflict as an opportunity to gain what they want by force, particularly if they are good at fighting. Many schools are now stressing the importance of building conflict resolution skills as a way of discouraging acts of violence.

Social factors also play a role in violent crimes. One of the greatest influences on violent crime is poverty. In areas of the United States where jobs are scarce and neighborhoods are poor, residents may feel that the only way to get what they want in life is to take it. The 2003 National Crime Victimization Survey found that for people in households earning less than $7,500 a year, 49.9 out of 1,000 people become victims of violent crimes, including robbery, murder, rape, and sexual assault. For those from households earning more than $75,000 a year, the victimization rate was only 17.5 per 1,000. Crime is simply more prevalent in poor neighborhoods. Guns are also more prevalent where poverty is high.

Alcohol and other drugs represent another social influence on violence. Simply put, people become less inhibited when they take drugs; they react to situations in ways they would not consider if they were sober. Of all the violent offenders in prison today, more than one-third were committed by individuals under the influence of alcohol or another drug at the time of the crime. In addition, people also commit crimes to *get* the drugs they want. Their addiction is so strong, the psychological and physical need for the drug so great, that they will commit acts of violence to obtain the money to buy drugs.

None of the personal, individual, or social influences mentioned thus far are single reasons someone turns to violence or commits a violent crime. In almost every case, a combination of factors influences a decision to engage in violence.

RISKY BUSINESS SELF TEST: TRUE OR FALSE?

Are you prone to violent behavior? Ask yourself the following questions. Keep a record of your answers on a separate piece of paper.

Question:	Yes, I do	No, I don't
■ I often engage in arguments with others.	_____	_____
■ I sometimes engage in arguments with strangers.	_____	_____
■ I sometimes lose my temper.		
■ I sometimes go to parties where alcohol and weapons are present.	_____	_____
■ I sometimes go to parties where some partygoers are strangers to everyone else present.	_____	_____
■ I drink alcohol and hang out with friends.	_____	_____
■ I carry a weapon in my neighborhood.	_____	_____
■ I carry a weapon at school.	_____	_____
■ I belong to a gang.	_____	_____
■ My behavior is easily influenced by my friends.	_____	_____
■ I get angry when others do not treat me with respect.	_____	_____
■ I am easily irritated or annoyed by others.	_____	_____
■ I make fun of others who are not like me.	_____	_____
■ I sometimes just need a good argument.	_____	_____

- I sometimes daydream about
  violent activity.   _____   _____
- I am easily angered while
  I am driving.   _____   _____
- I believe my boyfriend/girlfriend
  should do what I tell him/her.   _____   _____
- I most enjoy watching shows and
  playing games that have
  violent content.   _____   _____
- I will stay in an argument
  until I "win."   _____   _____
- I believe that most of the time
  my way of doing things is the
  right way to do things.   _____   _____

You may want to ask a person you trust to answer the same questions about your behavior as well. The hardest part of a self-test lies in being honest. Sometimes the way you see yourself is not how others see you. Compare your answers with a friend. If you find that your answers disagree or that you answered more than a few of your questions with "yes," you may want to learn more about violent situations and how they develop.

A TO Z ENTRIES

■ ABUSE, CHILD
See: Family Violence

■ ALCOHOL AND VIOLENCE
Alcohol is a mood-altering substance, one of the first used by humans, which can sometimes trigger violent behavior in certain people. Archeologists have found recipes for beer dating back 4,000 years to ancient Egypt and Sumeria. People who consume alcohol can have different reactions. They can become very quiet or very boisterous. In some cases, they become very aggressive.

Scientists and sociologists have studied the relationship between drinking alcohol and becoming violent for decades. They have found that people who use alcohol are much more likely to become violent than those who remain sober. The 1997 Alcohol Alert from the National Institute on Alcohol Abuse and Alcoholism offers statistics to support this conclusion: 86 percent of homicide offenders, 37 percent of assault offenders, 60 percent of sexual offenders, up to 57 percent of men and 27 percent of women involved in marital violence, and 13 percent of child abusers were under the influence of alcohol when they became violent.

Alcohol-related violence also has a financial cost. A 2000 report from the Department of Health and Human Services estimated that alcohol abuse cost the United States $184.6 billion in 1998. Those costs included $36.5 billion in lost earnings due to premature death, $9.1 billion for the lost work production of people imprisoned for alcohol-related crimes, and $1 billion in expenses for the victims of those crimes.

How does drinking alcohol encourage violence or make it easier for people to become violent? There is no simple answer. In truth, it may be a chemical change in their brains, a reaction to the environment, or simply what people expect to happen when they pick up a glass.

WHAT ALCOHOL DOES TO YOU
Alcohol is a drug classified as a **depressant**. A depressant is a drug that slows down the reaction time of the central nervous system. It impairs one's ability to react—a major reason why people should not drink and drive. A 1990 report by the Department of Health and

Human Services on the death toll from alcohol cited almost 20,000 fatal traffic accidents.

Fact Or Fiction?

Drinking lets people relax and blow off a little steam. It doesn't really hurt.

Fact: Some people relax when they drink, but others blow off a little too much steam. Of the 105,000 alcohol-related deaths categorized in a 1990 report by the Department of Health and Human Services, 9 percent were due to homicides and eight percent were due to suicides.

In its Campus Dating Violence Fact Sheet, the National Center for the Victims of Crime notes that when the victims knew the offender as a friend, classmate, or intimate partner, 75 percent of the men and 55 percent of the women had been drinking or using drugs before the sexual assault.

Many people incorrectly believe that alcohol is a **stimulant,** a substance that speeds up the central nervous system functions. Young people make this mistake because they feel more free, more open, and more talkative when they drink. Those feelings are a result of a reduction in inhibitions rather than an increase in functioning.

For example, if a young woman is normally shy, she might feel uncomfortable talking to a stranger, even though she might want to do so. Her anxiety tends to keep her from entering a situation that will cause her to be uncomfortable. Under the influence of alcohol, the young woman may be willing to take greater risks. Speaking to someone is not a great risk, but the same principle would apply if she were to decide to drive a car or deal with a conflict with a friend.

THEORIES ON THE LINK BETWEEN ALCOHOL AND VIOLENCE

Scientists have yet to establish exactly why violence increases when people drink. However, they have developed several theories on the link between alcohol and violence.

In 1996, scholars from the University of Southern California published a study in the *Psychological Bulletin* analyzing research on the links between alcohol and aggression. One explanation of violent behavior in people who have consumed alcohol is related to reduced inhibition. Consumption of alcohol reduces one's level of inhibition, possibly by reducing the amount of serotonin in the brain. Serotonin is a chemical in the brain that scientists believe monitors behavior.

Another theory notes that when people cannot attain a goal, they experience frustration. As the level of frustration increases, so does the level of violence. According to this theory, people who are intoxicated may evaluate situations differently than those who are sober. A problem that they might dismiss as trivial when sober becomes all-important when they are intoxicated. In other words, a person who has been drinking is more likely to overreact than a person who has not been drinking, and is therefore more likely to show aggression.

Q & A

Question: What do I do if I have a friend who drinks and gets violent?

Answer: No one wants to make a friend angry, but situations like this one really determine what kind of friend you are. First, never try to discuss the problem with your friend while he or she is drinking. Alcohol impairs one's ability to think, so there is little chance of a calm discussion.

If your friend begins acting violent, get yourself to a safe place. Wait until the person is sober to discuss the problem. Let the friend know how his or her drinking is affecting your relationship, and that violent behavior may cause greater problems down the road. If you can't discuss the problem with your friend, talk to a trusted adult. Your parent, their parent, or a teacher or school counselor may have good ways to intervene.

ALCOHOL, PERSONALITY, AND VIOLENCE

Some scientists believe there is more to alcohol-related violence than a simple chemical reaction. They add an additional aspect to the relationship—personality. A 2002 article in the journal *Psychology of Addictive Behavior* examined the relationship between those who have an aggressive personality and the likelihood of their becoming violent when drinking. The researchers found that "alcohol-related aggression was strongest among participants who desired an image of power." They also found that when individuals expect alcohol to make them more aggressive, or to show violence, then violence is more likely to occur.

CULTURAL EXPECTATIONS AND ALCOHOL

In much the way that differences in personality result in differences in the way individuals react to alcohol, cultural differences also play a role. A 1998 research paper by the Social Issues Research Centre points out that in some nations—including the United Kingdom, the Scandinavian countries, the United States, and Australia—people expect drinking to result in aggressive and violent behavior. In many Mediterranean countries and parts of South America, people have different cultural assumptions. There, intoxication is expected to result in peaceful behavior.

The report goes on to state that these differences cannot be accounted for by the amount of alcoholic beverages consumed or genetics. They seem to stem from different cultural beliefs about drinking alcohol, its effects, and what is appropriate behavior even while intoxicated.

A 1998 study reported in Marcus Grant and Jorge Litvak's book *Drinking Patterns and Their Consequences* discussed psychological experiments on individuals who believed they were drinking alcoholic beverages but actually were not. Researchers found that people's beliefs about their drinking had more effect on their mood and actions than what they had actually consumed. People who believed that drinking removes inhibitions became more outgoing. Those who believed that drinking puts one in a sexy mood became more amorous. People who believed that drinking results in violence became more aggressive.

Whether alcohol-related violence is a result of chemistry, psychology, sociology, or an interaction among the three, one point remains clear: People lose control when they drink. That loss of control often results in violence, and too often, violence adds to the 105,000 annual deaths attributed to alcohol by the Department of Health and Human Services.

See also: Criminals and Violent Activity; Media and Violence; School Violence; Teens and Violence; Violent Behavior, Causes of

FURTHER READING
Ojeda, Oriana, ed. *Teens at Risk: Opposing Viewpoints.* San Diego: Greenhaven Press, 2003.

■ ASSAULT AND BULLYING

Assault, a legal term for a threat or an attempt to harm another person, and bullying, a kind of assault that is intended to hurt or frighten another person. Bullying may or may not include physical violence. The behavior may consist of a physical attack but may also be limited to verbal bullying (calling a person names, teasing, and taunting him or her) and social bullying (excluding someone from a group or spreading malicious stories about the individual).

An important characteristic of bullying is the inequality of power between the bully and his or her target. The more powerful person or group attacks a less powerful individual.

Consider the following situations: A man knocks a woman down to steal her purse. In an argument over a girlfriend, one man threatens to kill the other, pushing him to the ground. A person tells a coworker, "If you tell the boss I left early, I'll have you fired." Each of these is a case of assault and may be considered a crime. Adults do not accept such behaviors.

Among young people, however, the distinction between an assault and bullying is often blurred. How would the following situations be viewed? A large boy forces other students to give up their lunch money. A new student is knocked down in the school playground because he or she looks "funny." Someone who has broken school rules about smoking threatens witnesses with painful or humiliating abuse if they say anything.

While these incidents are also examples of assault, they are more likely to be called bullying. Some people may even dismiss some of these incidents, saying things like "Boys will be boys," or "Some girls just go through a mean phase."

Since the 1970s, many psychologists have been focusing attention on bullying among young people. In 2001, the American Association of University Women did a comprehensive study of the issue, interviewing 2,000 public school students in the eighth through 11th grades. The teens reported that 83 percent of girls and 79 percent of boys had experienced harassment. According to the responses, 76 percent of the students experienced nonphysical harassment, while 58 percent had been physically attacked. In the same year, a study for the National Institute of Child Health and Human Development found that 29.9 percent of students in the United States were involved in bullying: 13 percent as bullies, 10.6 percent as their targets, and 6.3 percent as both bully and target.

WHAT BULLYING LOOKS LIKE

At any given time, children on a typical schoolyard may be squabbling, teasing, shoving, and even punching one another. How can an observer tell the difference between rough play and bullying? According to experts on bullying, the answer lies in whether a child repeatedly uses violence or threats to influence those around him or her. Experts look for a pattern of behavior.

Bullies also tend to target individuals whom they can continue to bully. They will force their victims to do the things bullies do not want to do or give the bully money. These behaviors generally mark male bullies. When girls bully, they use more indirect, less obvious methods. However, the impact can be just as damaging.

Fact Or Fiction?

All bullies are boys.

Fact: In 1995, researchers from Canada's York University videotaped children in two Toronto schools. In 52 hours, they recorded 404 bullying incidents, which lasted 37 seconds on average. The majority—72 percent—of the bullies were boys. However, girls were responsible for 28 percent of the bullying.

In her book *Odd Girl Out*, Rachel Simmons, who began her research on female bullying and the psychology of girls at Oxford University, views girls as less likely to punch anyone or knock someone down. Instead, girls use strategies like keeping their target out of the popular group, isolating her, spreading rumors, and damaging her reputation. An observer can often identify a target of female bullying as the girl who sits quietly, almost hiding among the boys, not because she wants to talk to them, but because she has been excluded from the circle of girls.

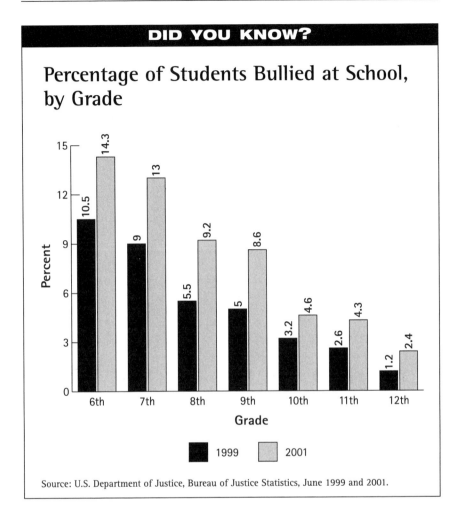

DID YOU KNOW?

Percentage of Students Bullied at School, by Grade

Source: U.S. Department of Justice, Bureau of Justice Statistics, June 1999 and 2001.

The female bully will glare at her target across the room, even as she chats with a friend. The impact of such behavior is hurtful to the person on the receiving end. The look says, "You are not wanted here." Feeling unwanted can be very painful, and for some girls (or people) it can take a lifetime to get over.

THE EFFECTS OF BULLYING

Repeated harassment takes its toll on a bully's victims. According to a 2003 study by Fight Crime: Invest in Kids, a national advocacy group, young people who are bullied are five times more likely to be depressed than other kids. Bullied boys are four times more likely than other boys to be suicidal and bullied girls are eight times more likely than other girls to be suicidal. The report also points out that 75 percent of the attackers in recent cases of school shootings were teens who had been victims of bullying.

Bullying also has consequences for the perpetrators, the individuals who bully. In his book *Understanding and Managing Bullying,* Delwyn Tattum cites a 22-year study which found that boys described by their peers as very aggressive (displaying bullying behavior) had a one in four chance of becoming criminals by the age of 30, compared to a one in 20 chance among other male students. The study also found that as these boys grew older, they acted aggressively towards their wives and children and tended to have children who behaved aggressively.

TEENS SPEAK

Mean Girls

Janet is a 21-year-old college junior. She was bullied by a group of girls all through high school.

"I was hated in school. I had bright red hair, was very skinny, and wore glasses. Nothing about me fit in with the 'in' crowd." Janet doesn't look up, keeping her eyes on her clasped hands. "And they let me know it. The girl who used to be my best friend quit talking to me because the cheerleading captain said it would not look good to be seen with a loser."

Her hands are tightly clenched together. "It turned out that a boy I really liked asked me out only because someone told him I'd do 'anything' to have him like me. When I wouldn't do 'anything,' he was gone. I spent most of my time alone because I was afraid of what people had said about me. By the time I was a senior, I just wanted to graduate and get away from there, because I thought it would be over. But it wasn't."

Janet's fingers are so tight, they've gone white. "I didn't see those girls after high school, but I felt so badly about myself that I couldn't get my life to work. At one point I even thought about ending it all, you know, committing suicide, but I couldn't do it. It took almost a year of counseling before I realized that I had some value, but it will take several more before I am over it, and I will never forget it."

DEALING WITH BULLYING

Are you a bully? To answer that question, take a hard look at yourself. Try to determine if you do things, say things, arrange things in such a way as to control others. People who bully make decisions about others based on what others have told them instead of what they know. Find out what others are like, and learn to accept that not all people will view the world the same way you do. That knowledge is part of becoming mature.

Perhaps you are not a bully but you support others who bully. You may occasionally be around when a friend or classmate is threatening others or spreading rumors. You have choices. You can ignore the behavior or suggest a different, more positive way to work out differences. Many people complain about peer pressure, the pressure or need to go along with others in a group. Making your disapproval plain is an opportunity to use peer pressure in a positive way.

Finally, learn how to resolve conflicts peacefully. It is a skill that can be learned in much the way you learn to shoot a basketball or sing. Like other skills, it also takes practice. Not only will it help you, but your friends will notice as well. It can be your chance to help create a better school for everyone. Things do not, and will not, change overnight and there will be those people who you simply cannot reach. Even so, at least you'll be making an effort to improve your corner of the world.

See also: Criminals and Violent Activity; Media and Violence; School Violence; Teens and Violence; Violent Behavior, Causes of

FURTHER READING

Carter, Jay, and Kathy Noll. *Taking the Bully by the Horns.* Pennsylvania: Unicorn Press, 1998.

■ COMMUNITIES AND VIOLENCE

Communities are groups of people who live in a particular local area, often bound together by economic, political, and social ties. How does violence affect communities? The World Health Organization (WHO), the global health authority of the United Nations, issued the World Report on Violence and Health in 2002. This study reported:

- 1.6 million deaths from violence
- 520,000 homicides
- 815,000 suicides
- 310,000 war-related deaths

North and South America, including the United States, had the second-highest homicide rate in the world. Like it or not, violence affects everyone. In many ways, individuals are products of their physical and social environments. A person's outlook and expectations are shaped by their home life and their neighborhood. The more violence a person lives with, the more profound are its effects.

A 1995 article in the *American Psychologist* discusses a situation called **chronic community violence** (CCV). Places marked by CCV have frequent and continuous exposure to the use of guns, knives, drugs, and random violence. Many of these places are poor, urban neighborhoods that have been compared to war zones. Like people trapped in a war zone, residents not only face the threat of physical harm, but also psychological danger.

Fact Or Fiction?

Crime is not just a problem in the inner city.

Fact: A 2004 report from the U.S. Department of Justice on school crime and safety found that 12- to 18-year-old students in urban areas were at greater danger of facing serious violent crime. For crimes like theft, however, the study found suburban students had a greater risk than urban students while in school, while students in rural areas had the same crime risk as urban students outside of school. Like it or not, crime—even violent crime—is everywhere.

COMMUNITIES THAT NEGLECT REPORTS OF VIOLENCE

According to the article in the *American Psychologist*, in areas where CCV is widespread, unchecked violence has a significant impact on those who live there. Children in such environments grow up believing that violence is a part of everyday life. Young children often cling to parents and caregivers, and may be fearful of exploring the world outside their homes. As they grow older, their early experiences with violence may encourage aggressive behavior. These young people may be more likely to respond to frustration with violence than young people in safer environments. Young people who grew up in violent surroundings may also have a nagging feeling that they do not "fit in" anywhere.

A 2003 study of youths in Los Angeles for the *Journal of Education* found that over 50 percent of the children in the neighborhood surveyed had been hit, slapped, or punched. Over 40 percent had been chased, threatened, or had hard objects thrown at them. More than 25 percent had experienced violence as a way of persuading them to do something they did not want to do. The researchers found that these children did not perform well academically. The more violence they had been exposed to, the lower their scores in school. Many suffered from depression and had low energy and even lower expectations of performing well in school.

The study identified students who were victims of violence as being more aggressive and less able to concentrate on schoolwork, again lowering their chances of academic success. Research published in the *Journal of Consulting and Clinical Psychology* in 2000 support these findings. These researchers found that youths who are victims of violence have trouble controlling their emotions, making them easy to anger. As a result they have much more difficulty making and keeping friends.

COMMUNITY VIOLENCE-PREVENTION STRATEGIES

Overcoming the negative influence of violence requires action from the entire community. The World Health Organization suggests several measures to increase safety and reduce violence at the community level, including:

- Utilizing public education to target communities or community entities like schools and businesses
- Modifying the physical environment by creating better lighting and safe routes to walk
- Ensuring the existence of after-school programs for youths
- Preparing police, health professionals, and educators to address violence with special training
- Developing community policing groups
- Coordinating efforts for a unified approach to dealing with violence

Using these strategies and others, cities across the United States have managed to reduce crime—and violence—in recent years.

WHAT CAN BE DONE

Some of these efforts are already under way in many communities, many of which have experienced success. Organizing a community to address violence means bringing many groups together. The 1997 guide *Building Coalitions 101,* issued by the advocacy group known as the Community Anti-Drug Coalition of America, offers a seven-step program to identify problems and to recruit help from parents and local service organizations. According to the Coalition, people in more than 5,000 communities are successfully working to reduce drug use and violence.

An example of creating coalitions from the national to the local level was the partnership between the American Psychological Association (APA) and MTV (Music Television) in the late 1990s to help prevent school violence. After a series of shootings at schools, the two organizations developed a program called Warning Signs. The effort was launched with the broadcast of a special documentary on MTV which featured a toll-free number that young people could call to request more information. The U.S. Secretary of Education helped promote the program to 60,000 educators, and APA members across the country joined in, offering community outreach. Psychologists in numerous cities and towns conducted youth forums and worked with church groups, boys and girls clubs, and other youth organizations. Special kits helped these volunteers prepare presentations and work with community leaders both to create grassroots activities and promote them.

Most efforts to address local issues are much smaller in scale, but the processes that enable their success are similar. Many communities also have support systems established to help individuals. Self-help groups are commonly found throughout the nation, with support in dealing with such issues as alcoholism and drug abuse, both of which can lead to violence. A look in the local phone book may reveal help lines for those who are coping with child abuse, sex crimes, or family violence.

For those having difficulty changing violent behaviors on their own, personal counseling is an option. Trained professionals can work with perpetrators of violence to assist in learning appropriate nonviolent methods of expressing feelings and opinions. Local health departments often offer counseling or programs to help those who wish to control violent behavior. Violence is a community issue, and it will take a community effort to make neighborhoods safe.

Q & A

Question: How can I reduce violence in my community?

Answer: Many people feel overwhelmed by the problem of violence. What can a single person do? Community action is about uniting the work of many individuals.

The National Youth Violence Prevention Resource Center suggests many ways in which young people can become involved in community-based action against violence. You could volunteer with existing organizations in your town or city. Check and see if your school or a community group already has programs to prevent or counter violence. Another opportunity is to work with local government, serving on planning boards.

If there are no existing organizations in your area, you may follow the lead of many young people by stepping into the gap and creating your own. The Office of Juvenile Justice and Delinquency Prevention offers a publication, *Youth in Action,* to help in such efforts. It's available online at http://www.ncjrs.org/html/ojjdp/publist2000/youth.html.

The Department of Justice also maintains the Kids and Youth Web site, http://www.usdoj.gov/kidspage, where you can see what young people around the country are doing. You can also contact the

National Youth Violence Prevention Resource Center through their daytime help line, 1-866-SAFEYOUTH (1-866-723-3968). These are just some of the possibilities for community action that you can take.

See also: Drugs and Violence; Gang Violence; Social Costs of Violence

FURTHER READING
Anderson, Elijah. *Code of the Street: Decency, Violence, and the Moral Life of the Inner City.* New York: W. W. Norton, 2000.

■ CONFLICT RESOLUTION
See: School Violence

■ CRIMINALS AND VIOLENT ACTIVITY
People who habitually break the law, often committing the crime of theft. While some forms of crime such as fraud do not require violence, for most criminals, violent behavior is part of the job.

LEGAL DEFINITIONS
The Federal Bureau of Investigation (FBI) maintains the Uniform Crime Reporting Program, an effort to generate nationwide crime statistics. In this annual report, the FBI divides violent crimes into four categories:

- **Murder and nonnegligent manslaughter:** the willful (nonnegligent) killing of one human being by another
- **Aggravated assault:** an unlawful attack by one person upon another for the purpose of inflicting severe or aggravated bodily injury. This type of assault is usually accompanied by the use of a weapon or other means likely to produce death or cause bodily harm. Attempts involving the display or threat of a gun, knife, or other weapon are included because serious personal injury is likely to occur if the assault is completed.

■ **Forcible rape**: forcing a person to submit to sexual intercourse against his or her will. Assaults or attempts to commit rape by force or the threat of force are also included. The category does not include statutory rape (a sexual act between an adult and a minor; by law no minor can consent to sex with an adult).

■ **Robbery**: taking or attempting to take something of value by force or by threat of violence

LAWS

Laws are the rules that govern a community. Criminal laws usually ban specific acts considered harmful to individuals and the community as a whole. These laws often specify punishments for offenders. Violent offenses usually fall into one of two classifications. **Misdemeanors** are lesser crimes. Offenses include theft of items of little value, disturbing the peace, simple assault and battery, drunk driving without injury to others, and public intoxication. Those convicted of a misdemeanor usually pay a fine or spend up to a year in jail. **Felonies** are more serious crimes, punishable by a term in a state or federal prison, with a minimum sentence of one year, and, in some cases, the death penalty

The number of laws, lawbreakers, and court cases in the United States is staggering. In the last 20 years, concern over the operation of the courts has led to new laws setting guidelines for the administration of the legal system.

In 1999, the Bureau of Justice Statistics released a report stating that violent offenders, on average, completed only 44 percent of their sentences, or 45 months out of an average 85-month sentence. Because of community demand for jail time for those convicted of violent crimes, many states began adopting **truth-in-sentencing laws**. These laws require that violent offenders finish at least 85 percent of their sentence. In the 1994 Crime Act, the federal government promised money for more prisons to states enacting this type of law. If criminals were going to be staying in prison longer, the state would need more room to house them. The first state to adopt a truth-in-sentencing law was Washington in 1984. Since that time, over half of the states have passed laws that mandate a minimum percentage of time to be served by persons convicted of violent crimes.

In response to the increase in violent offenses and drug-related crimes in the 1980s, and to address differences in how individual judges sentenced criminals for the same crimes, the federal government created **mandatory sentencing laws**. These laws provide judges in federal courts with guidelines for sentencing based on the seriousness of the crime, previous convictions for the crime, and whether the accused has been cooperative with the courts.

Concern over repeat offenders of serious crimes led to the "three strikes, and you're out" laws. These state statutes establish tougher sentencing for criminals who repeatedly commit felonies. In most cases, if the accused has been convicted of a third offense, he or she faces 25 years to life in prison without the opportunity for parole. Washington State passed the first of these laws in 1993. In 1994, California voters approved a similar measure. At present, 24 states have laws that aim at keeping repeat offenders in prison. Variations exist from state to state as to what types of crimes qualify for this sentencing. For example, in some states, all three felonies must be

DID YOU KNOW?

Estimated Average Time to Be Served under Truth-in-Sentencing Laws

Most serious offense	New Sentencing		Estimated Time to Be Served		
	Maximum sentence (years)	Minimum sentence (years)	85% of sentence	75% of sentence	50% of sentence
Violent offenses	104	73	88	78	52
Murder	253	214	215	190	127
Rape	140	72	119	105	70
Robbery	101	60	86	76	51
Assault	72	45	61	54	36

Note: Excludes life, death, and without-parole sentencing

Source: Truth-in-Sentencing in State Prisons, Bureau of Justice Statistics, 1999.

violent offenses. Other states require that the first two offenses be violent, while the third can be any felony. A federal "three strikes" law also exists for those convicted of federal offenses.

LAW ENFORCEMENT

The job of investigating crimes and apprehending the perpetrators falls on officers of various jurisdictions. The 2001 annual report of the U.S. Department of Justice counted 441,000 police officers in the nation. Over 200,000 additional officers served at the state level. The total cost of employing these officers was $36.7 billion, or an average of about $179 per resident. At the federal level, an additional 93,000 people were authorized to make arrests, representing dozens of different government agencies, including the FBI, Secret Service, Immigration and Naturalization Service, U.S. Customs Service, and Federal Bureau of Prisons.

In many towns of moderate size, a police department consists of a police chief, several officers, and various other professionals who have investigative or administrative duties. The amount of protection a local force can provide has a direct effect on the amount of violence in the community. The greater the protection, the less violence there was in the community. A 1996 study in the journal *Criminology* found that each additional police officer on duty in a city results in approximately 24 fewer crimes.

PUNISHMENT

After a lawbreaker is convicted in court, he or she is sentenced. Depending on the seriousness of the crime, and whether the case is in a county, state, or federal court, the judge will determine the appropriate sentence for the crime. In county court, the judge has considerable flexibility in determining what the sentence will be. One option is jail. If the crime is serious enough, a lawbreaker can typically be sentenced up to one year in county jail. Usually, if the crime is more serious, the case is tried in state or federal court, where a year's prison time is usually the minimum sentence.

Another sentencing option is **probation**—in which a convicted defendant is released under supervision as long as certain conditions are met. Probation has the requirement that if the person convicted of the crime gets into any additional trouble, the full sentence is enforced.

A third option is to have the lawbreaker pay a fine. The amount of the fine depends on the crime and usually includes an additional fee called court costs—the costs associated with the trial. Yet another sentencing option might be community service. Many judges will decide that rather than send a person to jail they will have him or her help make the community a better place. Some people who perform community service do menial jobs, such as picking up trash along the highways. More often, such service involves an assignment to work with a group of people connected to the crime. For example, a person arrested for drunk driving may be required to perform 100 hours of community service talking to youngsters about the dangers of drinking and driving, and the consequences they will face if they are caught.

When children and teens get in trouble with the law, they are tried in juvenile courts, state courts set aside for young people under the age of 18. (A few states, however, define juveniles as young people who are under the age of 16 or 17.) The goal of juvenile courts is to help young people in trouble rather than treat them as hardened criminals. Illinois established the first juvenile court in 1899.

In juvenile court, those found guilty of a crime are called delinquents. They are often released into the custody of parents or guardians and required to undergo counseling or do community service. When sentences are imposed, they are short, lasting only as long as the offender remains a juvenile. These sentences are usually served in juvenile facilities that emphasize rehabilitation. Juvenile records may also be sealed to protect the privacy of the young offenders.

Between 1985 and 1994, an increase in youth violence alarmed people nationwide, and many demanded changes in the juvenile justice system. Many states passed laws required that young people be tried as adults for serious offenses such as murder.

Crime often involves violence. Violent crimes influence laws, which in turn can seriously affect the lives of people, especially young people, who become caught up in the legal system.

See also: Drugs and Violence; Gang Violence; Homicide; Legal Interventions; Rehabilitation and Treatment of Perpetrators; Weapons of Violence

FURTHER READING
Dudley, William, ed. *Crime and Criminals: Opposing Viewpoints.* San Diego: Greenhaven Press, 1989.

■ DATING VIOLENCE
See: Teens and Violence

■ DOMESTIC VIOLENCE
See: Family Violence

■ DRUGS AND VIOLENCE

Substances taken into the body to treat a disease, affect one's mental processes, satisfy a dependence, or attempt suicide. The drugs most associated with violence, however, are illegal substances taken for their effect on the brain.

According to the 2003 Youth Risk Behavior Surveillance System, a government study of dangerous behavior by young people, 24.7 percent of American students have smoked **marijuana** in the last 30 days, 8.7 percent have tried **cocaine**, 12.1 percent have experimented with **inhalants**, 7.6 percent have used **methamphetamine**, and 3.2 percent of kids injected drugs intravenously.

A 1985 article in the *Journal of Drug Issues* set forth a three-point connection between drugs and violence, which was accepted by the National Institute of Justice (NIJ) as a basic concept in antidrug policies. This concept was subsequently used by the NIJ and the government to explain why drugs are dangerous. First, violence occurs because of the physical effects of drugs. Second is the economic compulsion–drug users often resort to crime to pay for drugs. Finally, the article identified **systemic violence**–essentially the cost of doing business in an illegal market. Disputes between drug dealers are often settled with guns, and the vast amount of unlawful cash draws robbers. Along with conflicts over price, selling of fake drugs, and run-ins with the law, the world of drugs is a violent place both for sellers and buyers.

Q & A

Question: Why does drug use seem to get out of control so fast?

Answer: One reason is tolerance—a physical reaction after being introduced to a drug. A user's system becomes accustomed to having the drug present and requires a larger dose to attain the effect of pleasure, or even to feel normal.

However, the more an addict uses a drug, the more the body needs. Eventually, the user is totally focused on attaining the drug, and any fun associated with drug taking disappears. Even with less addictive drugs, the users tend to become focused on thoughts and plans for the next time they will be getting high. At that point, users do not control the drug; the drug controls the users.

TYPES OF DRUGS

Illicit drugs fall into six groups. **Depressants** like chloral hydrate and pentobarbital slow the functioning of the nervous system. **Sedatives** like Valium and Xanax reduce anxiety in the user. (Alcohol also falls into this category.) **Stimulants** speed up the nervous system, raising heart rate and blood pressure. Cocaine, **crack,** and **Benzedrine** are all examples of stimulants.

Narcotics like codeine and morphine serve as painkillers in the medical field, but illegal drugs such as opium and **heroin** also belong to this group. **Cannabis** is another name for marijuana. Many teens consider marijuana to be harmless. Only 34.9 percent of young people considered monthly marijuana use to be highly risky, according to the government's 2003 National Survey of Drug Use and Health. In comparison, 64.7 percent of the respondents considered a pack-a-day cigarette habit to be highly risky. However, according to the American College of Emergency Physicians, cannabis distorts the senses, causes memory loss, damages the immune system, and, in some cases, creates hallucinations and fills users with paranoid fears. It also produces many of the same smoking hazards as cigarettes.

Hallucinogens, like LSD, PCP, and mescaline, distort reality, so that users see and hear things that are not really there. The effects of hallucinogens can last for hours, but the potential for flashbacks (reliving the experience at a later date without taking the drug) can last for years. The last group is **inhalants.** Anything sniffed is included in this group. Spray paint, glue, gas and cleaning products are common inhalants. Users feel dizzy and lightheaded. Inhalants may also stop heartbeat and respiration.

In a 2001 report, the Office of National Drug Control Policy estimated that in 2000, Americans spent $36 billion for cocaine, $11 billion on marijuana, $10 billion on heroin, $5.4 billion on metamphetamine, and $2.4 billion on other drugs. Totaling those figures offers nearly 65 billion reasons for violence in a hugely profitable criminal enterprise.

Fact Or Fiction?

Most kids try smoking pot in high school, so it's not a big deal.

Fact: Answering the 2003 Youth Risk Behavior Surveillance System survey, 40.2 percent of students in grades nine through 12 said that they had tried marijuana once or more. Nearly 60 percent *do not* smoke marijuana.

Smoking pot is a big deal. In 2003, the magazine *New Scientist* reported a study of twins. One of the pair began using marijuana before the age of 17, while the other didn't. The early users were two to five times more likely to use harder drugs or become dependent on alcohol than their nonusing twin. A 1994 study by Columbia University's Center on Addiction and Substance Abuse found that young people who used marijuana were 17 times more likely to use cocaine than young people who did not smoke pot.

INTRAVENOUS DRUG USE

Intravenous means inside or into a vein. One of the fastest ways to introduce drugs into the body is by way of the bloodstream. Drug addicts inject many substances, including narcotics such as morphine, Demerol, Percodan, Percocet, and dilaudid. The most common drug abused by intravenous injection is heroin. Some people feel that intravenous drug use has been glamorized by big-name rock stars like Jimi Hendrix and Janis Joplin and groups like Alice in Chains, Blind Melon, and the Red Hot Chili Peppers. Yet part of their fame (or notoriety) came from the fact that some of these musicians died as a result of their addictions.

Intravenous drug use is a very dangerous practice. Users expose themselves to the risks of disease transmission and **overdose.** Injected drugs like heroin can cause users to become highly agitated if their "high" is disturbed. The narcotic effect of the drug makes concentration difficult, leaving users easily startled. The way heroin affects the brain intensifies feelings of fear and suspicion, possibly triggering angry or violent outbursts.

Self-violence is also a real possibility. When a drug begins to wear off, the user may experience depression—a feeling of intense sadness and hopelessness. Such emotions have been known to lead to suicide.

TEENS SPEAK

Not a Good Buzz

Sean is a high school student who hopes to make up the class work for junior year—depending on the decision of his town's juvenile court.

"I thought I could handle it. We all did. It started in the ninth grade, smoking a little weed between classes in our friend's car. After a while though, that got boring, so we upped the ante."

He shakes his head. "The first time Freddie brought crack to school, we all looked at him like he was totally nuts. Smoking dope was one thing, but crack? No way. In the end, though, we did it."

Sean's lips twist as if he is tasting something nasty. "I was the last one. The guys were dogging me so much, I tried it just to make them shut up. It was the best high I'd ever had. So good, that I wanted to do it all the time. I thought I was in control, but the drug had me. We were all about finding the money to get some more rock."

He jams his hands into the pockets of his prison coverall. "We went to the next town over to hit the convenience store. Freddie held the gun while I grabbed the cash. I was already headed out the door when I heard the shot.

"So here I sit in Juvie, waiting on my trial. I just keep thinking, 'We were just getting a buzz, having some fun.' But it doesn't look that way now."

DRUGS AND LOSS OF CONTROL

When a drug user starts out, everything seems good—very good. For a small dose, often given free or for a low price, many users experience tremendous pleasure.

Even at that early stage, however, dangers exist. Drugs can impair the user's thought processes, leading to violence. The substances that commonly cause such reactions are stimulants like cocaine, alcohol, and hallucinogens like PCP. Another class of drugs that may cause physiological violence is steroids. Many young people, especially males, turn to these substances to build up muscle mass. However, a side effect of the drug is violent outbursts known as **steroid or 'roid rage.**

As time goes on, repeated doses of a drug lead to **addiction.** The user's body and mind are in constant need of the drug—not to feel pleasure, but to feel normal. **Tolerance,** the process by which the body needs larger and larger doses of a drug, sets in. The heavier the dose, the greater the cost an addict must pay.

If a user cannot get the drug, he or she may suffer from **withdrawal** as the body responds to the absence of what has become a necessary element. Symptoms range from restlessness and irritability to, in the case of heroin, life-threatening reactions. A person in pain and on edge can react unpredictably. As symptoms become more painful, an addict will do anything, including committing a crime, to raise the money for the next fix.

A group of researchers from the University of Delaware have explored the connection between drug use and criminal behavior among addicts in Miami for almost 20 years, as described in a 1998 article in the journal *Substance Abuse and Misuse.* Their study, begun in 1979, of 356 active heroin users found that nine out of 10 men sold drugs, seven out of 10 robbed, six out of 10 shoplifted, almost half carried out a robbery, 20 percent committed an assault, and almost 10 percent were responsible for acts of vandalism while using drugs. For women, eight out of 10 sold drugs, seven out of 10 shoplifted, more than seven out of 10 turned to prostitution, and almost 10 percent committed assault.

In 1993, at the height of the crack cocaine epidemic, the University of Delaware researchers studied the criminal activity of 611 young people. They found that 254 teens in the study were responsible for 223,439 crimes in the year preceding the study. Whether the crime turns violent is a reflection of what is happening during the commission of the crime. If the user gets nervous or the victim has a weapon, violence is more likely to occur.

Addiction means that users *must* buy drugs, and they must buy them from criminals, because the drugs are illegal. Law enforcement agencies target drug dealers, who are also targeted by business rivals. As an illegal cash business, drug sellers also attract other criminals hoping to get rich quickly. Unable to control their need for drugs, addicts deal with drug dealers. Like it or not, in doing so, the users put themselves in the cross fire of the violence that swirls around the drug business.

Drugs impair the judgment and sometimes create violent physical reactions. The need for drugs often drives users to crime. At the same time, the very act of buying drugs can put addicts in danger. However pleasurable, exciting, and glamorous the world of drugs may seem, its reality is very violent—and often deadly.

See also: Criminals and Violent Activity; Gang Violence; Social Costs of Violence

FURTHER READING
Avraham, Regina. *The Downside of Drugs.* New York: Chelsea House Publishers, 1988.

▓ FAMILY VIOLENCE

Violent activities that take place among members of a family. Because the violence usually takes place in the home, family violence is also called **domestic violence.** Family violence is a hard thing to talk about. Children do not want to admit that their mothers or fathers hit them, or that mother and father hit each other. It is hard enough to survive physical mistreatment. Adding social embarrassment to the violence is something most young people would prefer to avoid. But the fact is, family violence is a real problem that occurs regardless of whether a family is rich or poor, urban and rural, or a one-parent or two-parent household.

Fact Or Fiction?

When adults warn children about abuse, they should only warn them about strangers.

Fact: A 2000 study, *Sexual Assault of Young Children as Reported to Law Enforcement: Victim, Incident, and Offender Characteristics,* found that for juvenile victims (under the age of 18), only 7 percent of sexual assaults, according to the Bureau of Justice Statistics, were perpetrated by strangers. In 34 percent of the cases, the perpetrator was a family member, while 59 percent of the time, the victim somehow knew the perpetrator.

In its pamphlet *Child Protection,* the National Center on Missing and Exploited Children urges that parents train their children to watch out for certain types of behavior rather than certain types of people. To a child, a stranger is someone who looks unusual.

CHILD ABUSE

The U.S. Department of Health and Human Services (HHS) keeps track of child abuse on a national level. According to HHS statistics, nearly 1 million youngsters were abused or neglected in 2001. That number means for every 500 students in your school and others like it, six or seven children were probably abused last year. It happens to children of all ages, of all nationalities, and to both boys and girls. Generally, abuse of children involves **physical abuse, sexual abuse, emotional abuse,** or **neglect.**

The Committee on the Training Needs of Health Professionals to Respond to Family Violence has developed a number of definitions regarding abuse. Physical abuse is inflicting physical harm by punching, beating, kicking, biting, burning, shaking, or other actions that result in damage.

Sexual abuse is forcing children or adults who are unable to comprehend and/or give consent to engage in sexual activities. This abuse includes all forms of incest, rape, fondling genitals, and commercial exploitation through prostitution or the production of pornographic materials. Neglect is the failure of a loved one or caregiver to provide basic physical, emotional, medical, or educational needs.

The American Medical Association defines emotional abuse as threatening, humiliating, ignoring, or other emotional mistreatment of a child. This type of abuse includes the corruption of a child—for example, when adults introduce children to antisocial activities like crime, sexual activity or pornography, and drug or alcohol use.

A 2001 report from the National Child Abuse and Data System (NCANDS) revealed that parents were the most likely people to abuse children—they are responsible in 80.9 percent of abuse cases. According to 2002 statistics from the Administration for Children and Families, part of the HHS, more than 1,300 children die from abuse each year. Of the children killed, 76 percent were under the age of four.

Q & A

Question: If I am experiencing violence at home, who can I call for help?

Answer: If there is an adult in your life that you can trust, start there. If not, many organizations can help. A good place to start is by calling ChildHelp USA at 1-800-4ACHILD (1-800-422-4453). Your call will be kept confidential, and you can remain anonymous if you want. The group has people on the phones trained to give advice and to help you move forward with your life.

DISCIPLINE VERSUS ABUSE

Dictionary definitions of **discipline** range from "training to improve strength or self-control" to "punishment." Parents have long debated whether physical discipline, primarily spanking, is abusive. Some disapprove of any form of physical aggression toward a child. Others believe physical discipline such as spanking can be an effective way to get children to change their behavior.

According to the American Academy of Pediatrics (AAP), more than 90 percent of American families use spanking, which is defined as the use of an open hand "to a child's buttocks without causing injury, and with the intent to modify behavior of the child." In its policy statement, however, the AAP regards spanking as an ineffective strategy, with a potential for abuse. A 2002 article in *Psychological Bulletin* reports that two-thirds of incidents of parent-child abuse start out as an attempt at discipline.

Child neglect as a form of abuse

According to the 2001 NCANDS report, 59.2 percent of child abuse cases involve neglect. Neglect occurs when a parent or caregiver—like a grandparent or child-care provider—fails to meet the child's needs. The neglect may be visible, such as when a child is not fed on a regular basis and seems noticeably thinner than his or her peers, when he or she appears at school in torn clothing or missing pieces of clothing such as socks or shoes, or when the child's home is unsafe to live in.

Other forms of neglect may not be as visible. On religious grounds or due to other beliefs, some parents withhold medical care from a child. Other parents may believe that working and supporting the family takes priority over schooling, so the child may be removed from school at an early age. Today education is considered a basic need for all children. According to NCANDS in 2001, more than 450,000 children were found to be in situations where the adult responsible for caring for them withheld a basic need.

Intimate partner abuse
An intimate partner is an individual with whom an adult has a sexual relationship. The individual may be a current or former spouse, a live-in boyfriend or girlfriend, or a dating companion. Whenever these relationships result in physical, sexual, or emotional violence, they are considered instances of **intimate partner abuse.**

Women are the victims of intimate partner violence far more often than men. Department of Justice statistics for 2000 report that 20 percent of violent acts against women are committed by intimate partners. The 1998 National Violence Against Women Survey (NVAWS) conducted by the National Institute of Justice and the Centers for Disease Control and Prevention found that 24.8 percent of all women have experienced this form of violence at some point in their life. Men report similar violence, but in lesser numbers. In the NVAWS study, only 7.6 percent of men said they have experienced intimate partner abuse at some point in their lives.

In 2001, the University of California at Berkeley prepared training materials for professionals in the Child Welfare Service. These included lists of risk factors for domestic violence and severe violence. Among the risk factors are poor communication skills, quickness to irritation, and a rigid belief in traditional sex roles (a "macho" attitude).

Another major factor in marital violence is alcohol abuse. According to the University of California, about 60 percent of batterers abuse alcohol. Drinking impairs a person's ability to make sound decisions. In a troubled relationship marked by conflict, alcohol can lead to greater aggression and violence. A 2003 study in the *Journal of Consulting and Clinical Psychology* reported that on days when men engaged in heavy drinking, they were almost 20 times more likely to become violent than on days when they did not drink.

TEENS SPEAK

It's Hard to Be a Survivor...But What Choice Do I Have?

Jenna is a 19-year-old single mother. She's taking remedial classes and hopes to attend college.

"When I was six years old, the man my mother was living with began molesting me. I remember waking up one night to find him rubbing me all over, this stupid grin on his face. He kept coming to my room until I was 11. When my mother started to realize something wasn't right, she began sleeping in my room with me. But it was way too late; the damage was done."

Jenna shakes her head. "As I got older, Mom thought I was being rebellious. I just thought that smoking and drinking with my friends after school was better than going home. I met a boy my senior year in high school—I thought he was pretty cool. We would listen to music together or have a smoke. One day he invited me to his house to hang out. We were just listening to music and talking and the next thing I knew he was lying on top of me."

Her voice gets very low. "I didn't want sex, I didn't want to be touched. But I froze. Everything from the time I was very young rushed through my head, and I froze. I couldn't fight, or speak . . . I just lay there. When he was done, he told me not to be such a tease and to just relax. Less than a month later, I knew I was pregnant, but he was long gone."

Jenna takes a deep breath. "Now I'm trying to raise my little baby, and I've decided to talk about what happened. I see a counselor a couple times each month, and I am trying to make sense of it all—not that it's easy. There are good days and bad, but I owe it to myself, and now my child, to get my life on track."

ELDER ABUSE

Elder abuse is abusive acts against older persons—usually people over the age of 60. Social scientists only began studying this form of abuse in the 1970s. They now recognize that elder abuse includes

Persons Raped or Physically Assaulted in Their Lifetime, by Gender of Victim

Type of Assault	Percentage[a] Women (n= 8,000)	Men (n= 8,000)	Numbers[b] Women (100,697,000)	Men (92,748,000)
Total rape	17.6	3.0	17,722,672	2,782,440
Completed	14.8	2.1	14,903,156	1,947,708
Attempted only	2.8	0.9	2,819,516	834,732
Total physical assault	51.9	66.4	52,261,743	61,584,672
Threw something	14.0	22.4	14,097,580	20,775,552
Pushed, grabbed, shoved	30.6	43.5	30,813,282	40,345,380
Pulled hair	19.0	17.9	19,132,430	16,601,892
Slapped, hit	43.0	53.7	43,299,710	49,805,676
Kicked, bit	8.9	15.2	8,962,033	14,097,696
Choked, tried to drown	7.7	3.9	753,669	3,617,172
Hit with object	21.2	34.7	21,347,764	32,183,556
Beat up	14.1	15.5	14,198,277	14,375,940
Threatened with gun	6.2	13.1	6,243,214	12,149,988
Threatened with knife	5.8	16.1	5,840,426	14,932,428
Used gun	2.6	5.1	2,618,122	4,730,148
Used knife	3.5	9.6	3,524,395	8,903,808
Rape and/or physical assault	55.0	66.8	55,383,350	61,955,664

[a](n = number of people surveyed)

[b](Estimated number of men and women in the United States age 18 years and older)

Source: National Violence Against Women Survey, Centers for Disease Control and Prevention, 1998.

many different types of abuse, including those associated with child and spousal abuse (physical, emotional, sexual, neglect). However, elder abuse can also include **financial exploitation, abandonment, and self-neglect.** The American Psychological Association's Web site on elder abuse points out that in studies from 1994 to 2004, reported cases of elder abuse have consistently risen, from 117,000 to 241,000. The National Elder Abuse Incidence Study issued by the National Center on Elder Abuse (NCEA) in 1998 estimated that almost 450,000 older people are abused, with an additional 101,000 suffering from self-neglect. The NCEA also reports that roughly two-thirds of all elder abuse is committed by family members—either the victim's child or spouse.

CYCLES OF VIOLENCE

Attitudes about violence are established in childhood. The surgeon general, the nation's chief public health officer, issued a report on youth violence in 2001 that commented in part on 40 years of research and discussion on the impact that watching violence on television has on children. How much worse are the effects of seeing violence on a daily basis in real life? Children growing up in violent homes see their mother humiliated, battered, or sexually abused. They stand a chance of being beaten themselves.

How does that violence affect a developing mind? The answer seems to be that such children become desensitized to violence—they get used to it. A 2003 study of youths in Los Angeles published in the *Journal of Education* found that children who live with violence have poorer grades in school, less energy, and lower expectations for themselves than other children. Young victims of violence tended to be more aggressive and less able to concentrate on schoolwork. The results of a 2000 study published in the *Journal of Consulting and Clinical Psychology* suggest that youthful victims of violence have trouble controlling their emotions, easily become angry, and experience difficulty making and keeping friends.

A violent upbringing continues to affect children as they grow older. A study discussed in a 2002 edition of the *Journal of Marriage and Family* reviewed the responses of thousands of adults linking their memories of their childhood to the way they behave in relationships. Women who grew up in homes with parents who abused their children and each other were at a much greater risk both to abusing and being abused as adults. Men who grew up in such homes were twice as likely to abuse their partners in adult life in contrast to men who grew up in homes without family violence. While most men who were abused as children do not become abusive as adults, a 1996 study of 551 men in the *Journal of Traumatic Stress* found that 70 percent of all perpetrators of physical or sexual violence were abused as children.

Thirty years ago, when family violence first became a public concern, it was a very difficult aspect of American life to research. Today, it remains difficult for researchers to even define the scope of problem. Nearly every study on child abuse, domestic violence, and elder abuse cites a lack of firm figures because of underreporting. Whether from shame or because they can't believe they are actually in an abusive situation, many people keep silent when they are in trouble.

See also: Legal Interventions; Sexual Violence; Social Costs of Violence; Violent Behavior, Causes of

FURTHER READING
Brown, Isobel. *Domestic Crime*. Broomall, Pa: Mason Crest Publishers, 2003.

■ FIGHT OR FLIGHT RESPONSE

An instinctive reaction to danger or stress. The fight or flight response is a throwback to prehistoric times, when a split second could mean the difference between life and death, between being fed or feeding a predator. Today, this instinct plays a part in the way humans respond to conflict, frustration, and anxiety.

Few people encounter hungry wolves or bears today. They may, however, have to deal with an exam in literature class, a basketball game against a rival school, or an attempt to persuade a parent to reconsider a curfew. Among the bodily responses that accompany these experiences are a racing heart, sweaty palms, and heavy breathing. More extreme situations may produce dizziness or nausea. All of these reactions are normal, part of the fight or flight response.

When someone encounters a **stressor**—an item or situation that causes stress—the body prepares itself either to meet the challenge head-on or to come up with an escape plan and avoid it.

THE BIOLOGICAL RESPONSE

The fight or flight response does not involve the higher thinking parts of the brain. It comes from the **autonomic nervous system** (ANS), in the primitive parts of the brain, the spinal cord, and nerves in the chest area. The ANS runs functions that usually do not require conscious control, like digesting food, the pumping of the heart, and breathing.

When stress is detected, the ANS "revs up" body functions. Chemicals called **hormones** flood the system, preparing the body for sudden, extreme exertion. Among these body chemicals are epinephrine, known as the fear hormone, and norepinephrine, the anger hormone. A rush of emotions overpowers the thinking parts of the brain, which may explain why some students "melt down" on major tests. They literally cannot access the information they studied. Instinctive response may be necessary in a physical crisis, where action is needed rather than thoughtful debate. Unfortunately, modern sources of stress (like tests, job interviews, or traffic problems) cannot be resolved by running away or lashing out in anger.

In a physical sense, everyone reacts to stressful situations in the same way. Why are some people able to deal with the stress, while others resort to violence? The answer lies in the ability to manage the degree of anxiety connected with the stress.

THE HARDY PERSONALITY

In his 1999 address to the American Psychological Association conference, Salvatore Maddi reflected on his 20 years of researching what is called the **hardy personality.** Maddi and his colleagues discovered that three mental attitudes determine how well a person is likely to handle stress. These are commitment, control, and challenge.

An individual's level of commitment demonstrates a willingness to be involved with other people rather than being alone. Connections to others and to the world around him or her can help an individual handle stress in a more positive fashion. Control, says Maddi, involves "struggling to have an influence on outcomes." Those who maintain control do not respond passively or feel powerless. Finally, accepting the challenge of day-to-day living reflects a desire to learn from experiences rather than taking the easy way out or letting fear of a possible failure stop one from trying. Today these attitudes are referred to as the **three Cs of hardiness.**

The notion of hardiness helps explain why some people handle stress well, while others resort to violence. Individuals who believe they have some say in the outcome of life events and are willing to accept both success and failure are more likely to handle stress well. For some people violence becomes an expression of fear. They may dread the uncertainty of a situation or fear that it is beyond control.

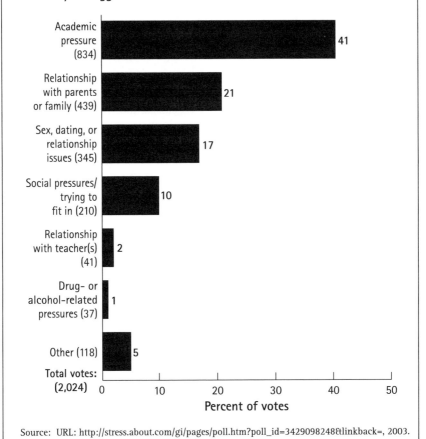

Stress Sources, As of 2003

About.com has maintained a running total of votes from teens on the stresses in their lives. The results are as follows:

What is your biggest source of stress?

- Academic pressure (834): 41
- Relationship with parents or family (439): 21
- Sex, dating, or relationship issues (345): 17
- Social pressures/ trying to fit in (210): 10
- Relationship with teacher(s) (41): 2
- Drug- or alcohol-related pressures (37): 1
- Other (118): 5
- Total votes: (2,024)

Percent of votes

Source: URL: http://stress.about.com/gi/pages/poll.htm?poll_id=3429098248&linkback=, 2003.

Acting out becomes a way to prevent change. Developing the three Cs of hardiness can help to reduce levels of anxiety, and, in turn, reduce the degree of violence. A major step in the right direction is working to change one's outlook or mood.

ENHANCING YOUR MOOD

When someone is observed acting in an aggressive way, people often comment that he or she "is in a bad mood." One's mood is a result of the complicated interaction of all body systems. However, according to a series of California-based research studies published in the *Journal of Personality and Social Psychology* in 1994, people can do a variety of things to enhance their mood. The California researchers defined a good mood as a high state of energy combined with a low state of tension. Unfortunately, many everyday events cause stress and lower one's energy. The California researchers found that people have the means to change their mood.

Mental approaches

- **Communication.** Most participants in the California studies reported that sharing what was bothering them with another person helped to restore a positive mood. Calling someone, sitting down to talk, or just being with someone they trusted helped to reduce the level of tension they felt.

- **Positive self-talk.** A lot of background chatter goes on in the human brain—fragmentary thoughts, observations, even things people unconsciously overhear. This flood of information can increase tension. Making a conscious effort to add positive comments to this stream of interior conversation can have a positive effect on energy levels. Perhaps it seems corny for people to give themselves a pep talk. However, reminders that they do not have to be perfect, that even failure can teach something, or that a recent argument does not mean the end of the world can help to refocus their attention on the positive.

- **Problem solving.** Sometimes the most obvious solutions are the ones most likely to be overlooked. People need to take time to determine why they feel stressed. What steps led to the anxiety? Could the conflict have been avoided if they had acted differently? What might they do differently if confronted with a similar situation in the future? Examining problems requires self-honesty. People always find it easier to note what others did wrong than assess their own mistakes.

Behavioral approaches

- **Exercise.** The hormones triggering the fight or flight response can be burned off through vigorous exertion. Many participants in the California studies identified physical activity as their top method of enhancing their energy and reducing stress. Health professionals have known for a long time the benefits of regular activity. Exercise does not require participants to run a marathon or join an aerobics class at a health club. Simply walking around the block or even active gardening can get the body moving and increase the level of wellness.

- **Music.** Participants in the California studies surprised researchers by rating music as an effective way to relieve tension and increase energy. A favorite CD can serve as a momentary distraction from a current issue. Music also allows people to regain their composure and thoughts while doing something they enjoy.

- **Rest.** The *Merck Manual of Medical Information* states that healthy adults may need as little as four or as many as nine hours of sleep every day. No matter how much an individual needs, sleep allows the body to regain energy and heal itself. If one is running on empty, the best response might be to call it an early night or catch a quick nap during the day (but not in class).

What does not work

While there are many things that can help restore energy and reduce tension, the California studies found that a number of common methods were not effective. These included:

- **Being alone or avoidance.** Sometimes people find it good to be alone for short periods of time to regain their thoughts or calm themselves. However, being alone in order to avoid a situation does not work. Conflict will not resolve itself without an effort. It takes some courage to face a challenge, but like any other skill, practice at facing problems makes the job easier.

- **Eating.** Many people use food as a comforting tool. Using food as a distraction to avoid a conflict only creates health problems down the road and may even lead to eating disorders.

■ Television. One of the easiest ways to disconnect from the world is to turn on the television. Like other distractions, using the television comes down to a question of purpose. Watching TV to give oneself a break and calm down is okay. However, when sitting in front of the television becomes the means of avoiding larger issues, it is time to face the challenge.

The fight or flight response is hardwired into every human brain and can be a powerful incentive to violence. Learning to control one's reactions to this instinctive drive may be a difficult job. However, it can be achieved, resulting in a better quality of life both personally and for those around one.

See also: Road Rage; Violent Behavior, Causes of

FURTHER READING
Casey, Carolyn. *Conflict Resolution: The Win-Win Situation.* Berkeley Heights, N.J.: Enslow Publishers, 2001.

■ GANG VIOLENCE

The violent behaviors of a group of people, usually young, who often band together for criminal purposes. A 1997 article in the *Journal of Gang Research* maintains that gangs are marked by an organized structure, criminal behavior as a focus of activity, and the use of symbols or rituals to reflect members' affiliation.

Gang activity is often violent because gangs commonly engage in lawbreaking, such as robbery, shaking down local businesses, car theft, weapons violations, and selling drugs.

Another source of violence is conflict with other gangs. As gangs develop, they usually stake out an area as their territory, or **turf.** Depending on the number of members and the degree of organization, gang turfs can include an entire neighborhood or a smaller area such as a particular housing project, a strip mall, a school, or a park. Whatever the space, gang members consider it forbidden ground for members of other gangs. Intruders face physical attack or worse, which leads to retaliation and sometimes escalates to outright gang wars.

One way gang members carry on conflict is through **drive-by shootings,** murders committed when one gang member drives a car past a group of rivals while another fires a weapon into the crowd. Such attacks often result in the death or injury of innocent bystanders.

THE CHANGING FACE OF GANGS

According to a 1998 article in the *Juvenile Justice Bulletin,* writers have been describing gang-like behavior among young men in American cities since 1783. Social scientists did not begin to study street gangs until the 1920s, and gangs did not become a concern of the general public until the 1950s. Movies like *The Wild One* portrayed motorcycle gangs, while *The Blackboard Jungle* showed an urban, school-centered gang. *West Side Story,* a Broadway musical turned hit film, featured an urban gang war.

In the 1950s, gang members were considered "juvenile delinquents." People expected them to outgrow gang behavior. However, many gangs have not faded away. The Vice Kings in Chicago were organized in the 1950s and still recruit members today. Since the 1980s, a number of gangs have also enlarged their geographic spread, starting operations in other cities. The 1998 article in *Juvenile Justice Bulletin* points out that in the 1980s, gang membership changed, with a greater number of both older and younger members. Gangs began to have *veteranos,* members who have belonged to the gang for 18 years or more.

The 1980s also marked major media exposure for gangs and the gang lifestyle. Coverage of the ongoing street war between the Crips and the Bloods in Los Angeles placed those two organizations center stage, making their blue and red identifying colors known nationwide. In some areas, local gangs began adopting similar names and colors.

In discussions about colors, tattoos, and graffiti, people often overlook a number of groups. **Skinheads,** groups that promote racial supremacy, are also considered gangs. These young people are looked on as the "frontline warriors" for organizations like the Ku Klux Klan and the White Aryan Resistance. Left-wing gangs, like Straight Edge, vandalize fur and furniture stores in the name of animal rights.

TEENS SPEAK

One Shot from the Edge

Neal is 19 years old. He ran with a gang for three years.

"So there I was, walking down the street with a gun down my pants. My gang, the Playboys, sent me out to kill a guy from the Kings. He'd shot some of our brothers while they were on the way to mess up a Kings' party. One of our guys had to ditch the machete he was carrying before they took him to the emergency room."

Neal shrugs as he looks back. "I realized this was getting pretty heavy. I'd been with the gang for three years, since my family got—what do they call it? Dysfunctional. Dad split, Mom worked, and I started hanging with the Playboys.

"While I was looking for that guy from the Kings, the gun I was carrying just got bigger and heavier. I was tight with one guy who'd shot somebody. They'd dissed him in the street, and the other brothers kept dogging him until he took out a gun and shot the guy."

His face gets very tight. "We all ran, but my buddy got caught and ended up being put away for a long time. I hear he curses the day he ever carried a gun.

"Maybe it's lucky I was alone. If the brothers had been dogging me, I might have gone through with it. Instead, I ended up throwing the gun in a sewer. I went home, started dressing like a regular person—no colors. I've got a job, and I'm working for my GED."

Neal shakes his head. "Now I've got a shot at having a life—instead of having it end because I shot somebody, or somebody shot me."

ACCEPTANCE BY A GANG

Why would a young person embrace a violent and dangerous lifestyle? Often they live in dangerous and violent neighborhoods. In the *Juvenile Justice Bulletin* article, many gang members cited protection as a major reason for joining. A 1995 national survey of young people between the ages of seven and 17 by Children Now and the Kaiser Permanente Foundation revealed another reason. About 62 percent of the young respondents believe that people join gangs for a sense of belonging. Many young people enter gangs in search of the close family relationships that seem to be missing from their own family life.

Many gangs are good at convincing potential members to join. The Comprehensive Community Reanimation Process, published by Urban Dynamics, Inc., spells out many of the techniques used by gangs to recruit members. Often, current members will tell tales of glory and spectacular lifestyles to convince young people that the gang is the place to be. The image of driving an expensive car with lots of money in one's pocket and an arsenal of weapons in the trunk has a powerful lure for some teens even if they suspect that the picture the gang paints is untrue or unrealistic. A sense of obligation can be yet another strong influence on young people. Essentially, gang members say, "If I do you a favor, then you owe me, and my 'fee' is your loyalty to the gang."

The media also plays a part in encouraging young people to join gangs. As early as 1961, big-budget movies portrayed gang involvement. While the dancing gang members in *West Side Story* may seem old-fashioned to today's young audiences, the characters have cool nicknames, hang out at a local store, and do not go to school. To some people, that sounds like fun. More recent films such as *South Central* and *New Jack City* show a harder-edged view of the drugs and violence associated with gangs, but still present the tight connection among gang members in a favorable light. For a young person with a difficult home life, the notion of gaining a family may outweigh the drug and violence issues.

THERE ARE NO GANGS HERE . . . ARE THERE?

The majority of young people who join gangs feel cut off from their family or their community, and the sense of belonging to a group that will love them and protect them is powerful. This disconnected feeling used to be attributed to poor family structures in the inner city. Therefore, gang activity has long been considered an urban problem. It was thought that only big cities like Los Angeles, New York, and Chicago had gang problems, not small towns or rural areas. Today, law enforcement officers and researchers are aware that gangs are no longer an urban problem. For many reasons, young adults feel alienated. Membership in a gang has become a way for many of them to find security.

In the 1995 book *The American Street Gang,* author M.W. Klein shared his research on gang growth. In 1960, only 58 cities reported gang activity. By 1980, 179 cities reported gangs, and by 1992, that figure had risen to 769 cities.

In 2001, the *Report on the Growth of Youth Gang Problems in the United States, 1970–1998* was issued by the Office of Juvenile Justice and Delinquency Prevention. According to this report, 201 cities reported gang activity in the 1970s. That figure rose to 468 cities in

DID YOU KNOW?

Risk Factors at Ages 10–12 for Gang Membership

Potential Childhood Risk Factor	Percent of Youths Who Join Gangs*
Neighborhood	
Availability of marijuana	30
Neighborhood youths in trouble	26
Low neighborhood attachment	20
Family	
Poverty (low household income)	23
One parent in home	21
One parent and other adults in home	25
No parents in home	24
Parental alcohol intake	15
Sibling antisocial behavior	22
Poor family management	21
Parental pro-violent attitudes	26
Low attachment to parents	20
School	
Low academic aspirations	20
Low school commitment	21
Low school attachment	23
Low academic achievement in elementary school	28
Identified as learning disabled	36
Peer	
Association with peers who engage in problem behaviors	26

* Percentage of youths joining a gang among youths who had scored in the worst quarter on the risk factor at ages 10-12

Source: Office of Juvenile Justice and Delinquency Prevention, 1999.

the 1980s, and to 1,487 cities by the mid-1990s. The report also viewed gang growth in terms of the counties affected. In 1970, the counties with gang activity represented 35.6 percent of the total population of the United States. By 1995, 77.9 percent of the population lived in counties with gang activity.

The National Youth Gang Survey issued by the Department of Justice estimated that there were more than 24,500 gangs in 2000, with members in excess of 772,500. The New York Police Department's gang intelligence unit reported that gangs were operating 95 percent of the large cities in the United States and 88 percent of the smaller ones.

Speaking to the 1996 conference of the Violence Intervention and Prevention Institute (VIP), Michael Walker of the Partnership for a Safer Cleveland discussed conditions that seem to foster gang growth. Any region where factories and other businesses are closing and the unemployment rate is disproportionately high has an increased chance of seeing gang activity develop.

Another major change in gangs involves girls. A 1998 article in *Crime & Justice,* an annual review of research, reports that it is difficult to get an accurate picture of the degree of female involvement in gangs. Police tend to underreport data on female gangs. As a result, police statistics suggest that women are responsible for only about 5 percent of gang activity. However, the article notes that additional information produced by researchers suggests that up to one-half of all gang members are girls.

GANGS AND SCHOOLS

The culture of many high schools is a good fit for gang activity. High schools are filled with young teens trying to fit in, to join a welcoming group to which they can relate—exactly what gang members tell them a gang can offer. As a result, in communities where illegal drug sales are high, the school may become a battleground with gangs fighting to corner the market.

Based on what is known about why youths join gangs, schools can discourage gang membership by creating an environment where students feel welcome and educators help students feel as though they belong. Speaking on gang prevention at the 1996 VIP Institute, Walker identified the following as important lessons that should affect the way schools are run:

- Focus activities on nine- to 12-year-olds, before they have an opportunity to join a gang and while they are not yet adolescents

- Start programs early and continue them throughout a child's years in school

- Ask young people to play a role in the development of activities and policies that help teach and reinforce the skills that discourage gang activity

- Remember young people are individuals—they do not all think, act, or behave in unison and should not be treated as though they do

- Get families involved

- Encourage local business leaders and organizations to assist the school in providing activities that meet the needs of students

- Keep school-based activities connected to local organizations. Resources can be pooled and children can be more easily networked in the community through preexisting relationships

A 1997 article in the *Journal of Gang Research* argues that schools need to recognize the signs that gangs are being formed in order to prevent their activity in the school. Researchers suggest that schools start by identifying students who may fit the gang member profile.

Which students show signs of needing the type of support a gang claims to provide? In his 1995 book, *The American Street Gang*, M. W. Klein suggests that gang members are not very different from their non-gang peers. However, gang members do tend to demonstrate some of the following attributes to a greater extent when contrasted with non–gang youths:

- Difficulty with school work, often having lower than normal IQs

- Poor impulse control

- A marked tendency toward aggressiveness and physical prowess

- Inadequate social skills

- An enhanced need, or desire, for belonging

- An enhanced need, or desire, for status and recognition
- A boring, uninvolved lifestyle in which episodes of excitement are sought and valued
- A weak or nonexistent attachment to adult control systems
- A lack of structure to develop personal and social identity

Once school officials have determined which students are most vulnerable to gang influence, they also need to watch for symbols of gang membership. Are distinctive patterns of color showing up in some student circles? Has graffiti appeared on the school grounds? School personnel should be trained to recognize how gang development looks. Most importantly, the staff needs to enforce school rules in a consistent way. Officials also need to work with students to develop communication and conflict resolution skills to reduce violent outcomes in conflict situations.

Gangs have appeared in all 50 states, in almost every racial and ethnic group, in a variety of social and economic situations, in large cities and small towns. Experience has shown the problems associated with intervention—trying to get young people out of gangs once they have become established is difficult. Yet preventing gangs from organizing in the first place is an important step in reducing the threat of violence for young people in their homes, neighborhoods, and schools.

Q & A

Question: I don't want to be in a gang any longer. How can I get out?

Answer: With some gangs, it's easy to get in and get out. With others, getting out can be difficult and even dangerous. The National Alliance of Gang Investigators Associations offers this advice:

- Never tell the gang that you plan to leave—you may be beaten or even killed.
- Stop hanging around with gang friends and find something else to do—sports, clubs, school or family activities.

- Stop dressing and talking like a gang member.
- Become good at making excuses—when gang members call, you have to be either away or busy doing something else. With luck, this will allow you to "fade away" from the gang.
- Find people who will believe in you and will help you by offering support and good advice.

Leaving a gang may be a struggle, but it will let you escape from a dead-end street and win your life back.

Fact Or Fiction?

Being in a gang protects me while I live in a violent neighborhood.

Fact: It might seem like a good idea to have a gang to watch one's back in a dangerous neighborhood. The National Alliance of Gang Investigators Associations points out, however, that becoming a gang member makes a person a target for rival gangs. Gang members face an increased risk of being injured or killed. The simple act of leaving their neighborhoods exposes them to danger. Even if they succeed in leaving a gang, their former rivals can still make dangerous enemies.

See also: Assault and Bullying; Media and Violence; School Violence; Teens and Violence

FURTHER READING
Cozic, Charles P., ed. *Gangs: Opposing Viewpoints.* San Diego: Greenhaven Press, 1996.

■ GUN USE
See: Criminals and Violent Activity; School Violence; Weapons of Violence

■ HATE CRIMES

According to the U.S. Department of Justice, violence intended to hurt and intimidate someone because of his or her race, ethnicity, national origin, religion, sexual orientation, or disability. Examples of hate crimes in the news in the past years include the slashing of car tires in a predominantly Jewish neighborhood; a Sikh restaurant owner being taunted as a terrorist, then beaten because he wore a turban; an African American dragged to his death after being chained to a pickup truck; and a gay man severely beaten, tied to a fence, and left to die.

No two human beings are exactly alike. People differ in countless ways from one another, including interests, abilities, skin color, religion, sexual preference, neighborhood, and family wealth. For some people, those differences become a way of distinguishing themselves from others.

According to many psychologists, although it is natural to see oneself as an individual and view others as representatives of groups, **stereotypes** are offensive. They are more than a label or judgment about an individual based on the characteristics of a group. Stereotyping reduces individuals to categories. Therefore stereotyping can lead to **prejudice** and **discrimination**. The word *prejudice* means "prejudge." People prejudge when they have an opinion about another person based on his or her membership in a particular group. A prejudice attaches value to differences to the benefit of one's own group and at the expense of other groups. Discrimination occurs when prejudices are translated into actions. When those actions become violent, they are considered hate crimes. Not every stereotype results in discrimination, but all stereotypes tend to divide a society into "us" and "them."

In their article on hate crimes in the *Encyclopedia of Peace, Violence, and Conflict*, Northwestern University professors Jack Levin and Jack McDevitt point out that since the 1980s, some members of majority groups have viewed efforts to end discrimination as challenges to their own status. These individuals view dramatic increases in interfaith and interracial dating and marriage as a threat. They are also troubled by newly arrived immigrants from Latin America and Asia. They are uncomfortable with racial integration in their neighborhoods, schools, and workplaces. They are outraged by the number of gay men and lesbians who have "come out" and, in many cases, begun organizing for equal status in their communities. Hate crimes are the responses of certain members of the majority to such perceived threats.

THE MENTALITY BEHIND THE HATRED

Many would like to believe that the people who commit hate crimes are hate-crazed extremists. Research at the University of California, Los Angeles, reveals that of 1,459 hate crimes committed in the Los Angeles area from 1994 to 1995, fewer than 5 percent of those responsible belonged to organized hate groups. Most offenders were otherwise law-abiding young people who saw little wrong with their actions. Alcohol and drugs sometimes fueled hate crimes, but in general, people who commit hate crimes believe that the society as a whole gives them permission to attack certain groups.

In a 1997 Congressional Briefing on hate crimes, psychologist Karen Franklin discussed a study of 500 people from the San Francisco area. About 10 percent of the subjects admitted physical violence or threats against people whom they believed to be gay. Another 24 percent reported antigay name-calling. Among men, 18 percent admitted to acts of violence or threats of violence, with 32 percent resorting to name-calling. An additional 30 percent stated that they would react aggressively if a gay person flirted with or propositioned them.

The study examined the motives in antigay crimes and found four:

- Self-defense. Attackers saw sexual propositions as aggressive acts by gay predators.
- Ideology. Attackers acted from negative beliefs about homosexuality, often seeing themselves as defending traditional values.
- Thrill-seeking. Attacks resulted from a desire for excitement or to feel strong.
- Peer dynamics. Attackers joined others to prove their toughness or heterosexuality to friends.

At the same briefing, Donald Green, an expert on hate crimes, noted that such crimes often occur when minorities move into previously all-white areas. The offenders frequently justify their actions as defending a rapidly disappearing traditional way of life. Green also discussed this "defended neighborhood" excuse in a

1997 study for Yale University's Institution for Social and Political Studies.

The Encyclopedia of Peace, Violence, and Conflict points out that hate crimes are crimes with a message. That message is aimed not only at the victim but also at people *like* the victim. In fact, a 1995 study of hate crimes in Boston reported in *Klanwatch Intelligence Report* showed that 66 percent of the people committing the crimes did not know the victims. A rock through a window is not merely an act of vandalism, but a notice that an entire group is not welcome in a community, a workplace, or school.

Hate messages also go out over the media. In the book *Waves of Rancour: Tuning in the Radical Right,* authors Robert Hilliard and Michael Keith point out that more than 1,000 groups, usually calling themselves patriotic, denounce immigration, racial integration, and warn of "an international Jewish conspiracy" to take over the world, spearheaded by control of American finance and Hollywood. This propaganda is promoted in high-tech ways, from CDs for skinhead rock bands to the Internet. Entering "Jew" in the popular search engine Google gives an address for an anti-Semitic Web site in the top 10 responses.

Even the mainstream media can spark hate crimes. When a New York City talk-radio host launched a particularly sharp attack on immigrants from India who were moving into a New Jersey town in 1996, numerous ethnic slurs were spray-painted on Indian-owned homes and businesses the next day. Shots were even fired through the windows of one home owned by recent immigrants.

WHO ARE THE VICTIMS?

The victims of hate crimes in the United States are groups that are seen as different from the majority. Racial and religious minorities, homosexuals, and immigrants are often targeted. According to statistics collected by the U.S. Department of Justice (DOJ), 7,462 hate crimes took place in 2002. Of those crimes, 3,642 were racially motivated, 1,426 were based on religion, 1,244 on sexual orientation, and approximately 1,102 on national origin.

The previous year, 9,730 hate crimes were reported. Part of the reason for the higher number was a surge in anti-Islamic crimes after the terrorist attacks on New York City and Washington, D.C., in 2001. From 28 attacks on Muslims in 2000, the number rose to 481 in 2001.

DOJ hate-crime statistics have been collected from law enforcement agencies across the country since 1991. That year, 4,558 hate crimes were reported by 2,271 law enforcement agencies. By 2001, 11,987 police agencies were submitting reports on 9,730 incidents.

While more agencies now take part in the program, it still does not cover all hate crimes. Police departments differ in defining a hate crime and recording these crimes. A 1997 DOJ report, *A Policymaker's Guide to Hate Crimes,* suggests that crimes may be underreported. In cases of attacks on gays, many, especially those who have not "come out," are fearful of reporting an attack. Immigrants, especially those who have entered the country illegally or come from a country where the police are seen as the enemy, fear deportation if they report a hate crime.

When nonpolice organizations gather hate-crime statistics, the numbers are larger. In 1994, the Anti-Defamation League recorded 2,066 cases of anti-Semitic violence, harassment, vandalism, and violence. The FBI reported 908. That same year, the FBI reported 209 hate crimes against Asians and Pacific Islanders, a drop from the year before. Legal advocates for this group disagreed with that number. They reported 452 incidents, a sharp increase from the number reported the previous year.

Some suggest that advocacy groups may tend to overcount, but even the DOJ believes that its figures underrepresent the problem of hate crimes.

WHAT CAN BE DONE?

Hate crimes are, by definition, crimes. Whether someone attacks a person to steal a wallet or because the individual is different, the perpetrator is still guilty of a crime. Most states have laws against hate crimes, often adding extra penalties, such as additional prison time, for crimes motivated by hate. These laws have been challenged in the courts, but the Supreme Court has upheld the concept.

The effort to legislate against hate-inciting speech has proven more controversial. Canada and many European countries, including Britain and Germany, have laws that ban hate speech. The United States, however, protects such speech in the First Amendment to the Constitution.

State laws have tried to attack hate speech by banning **fighting words,** forms of expression designed to enrage listeners and incite violence. The courts have struck down most of these laws, because the language of these laws is too vague.

Criminologist Jack Levin took a more concrete view in a 2003 speech to students and faculty at Rhode Island College. He pointed out that most hate crimes are not committed by members of organized hate groups, but by young people who live nearby. Many people are bystanders during a hate crime. By not speaking out, they silently give permission to the criminals.

Levin challenged his audience to stand up for the people who have been targeted. He ended his speech by telling his listeners, "Please don't forget where hate begins, and that is in the silence of ordinary people."

See also: Gang Violence; Media and Violence

FURTHER READING

Levin, Jack, and Jack McDevitt. "Hate Crimes." In *Encyclopedia of Peace, Violence, and Conflict*. New York: Academic Press, 1999.

▓ HOMICIDE

The killing of one human being by another. In the eyes of the law, homicide is not always a crime. According to *Black's Law Dictionary,* the word *homicide* is a legally neutral term. Although **murder** and **manslaughter** are crimes, a person may kill in self-defense or to stop an escaping criminal. Homicide is also justifiable if taking a life is a part of one's duty as a prison executioner, for example. **Excusable homicide** occurs when the killing has no criminal intent. For example, a person who kills an attacker has committed excusable homicide.

Unlawful killing is called **felonious** or **criminal homicide.** Both murder and manslaughter fall into this category. To convict a person of a murder requires proof of planning and intent to do harm. It has to be a "willful" act. Manslaughter is murder without intent. Manslaughter can be voluntary, such as a deadly fistfight, or involuntary, such as an accident caused by a speeding car. Like murder, both voluntary and involuntary manslaughter are considered criminal homicides.

Fact Or Fiction?

Murders are the most committed crimes.

Fact: Murder may seem to be the most common crime, if you read mystery novels or watch films and TV dramas. However, murders make up the smallest category of violent crimes in the FBI's Uniform Crime Reporting Program. In 2002, law enforcement agencies across the country reported 16,204 murders. In the same period, they reported 95,136 forcible rapes and 420,637 robberies. Cases of aggravated assault—attacks with a weapon or attempts at great bodily harm—totaled 894,348.

THE EXTENT OF CRIMINAL HOMICIDE

According to a fact sheet on leading causes of death from the Centers for Disease Control and Prevention, homicide was responsible for 7.1 percent of American deaths in 2003. The report also noted that homicide was "not ranked as one of the top ten leading causes of death, but a leading source of death in certain demographic groups."

The Bureau of Justice Statistics reported 14,080 homicides in 2002, continuing a downward trend in recent years. In fact, the overall rates in 2000 were as low as they were in the 1960s. Not all of the news is good, however. While African Americans make up about 14 percent of the total U.S. population, they accounted for 52.1 percent of the offenders and 46.8 percent of the victims of homicide in 2002. They were six times more likely to be a victim of criminal homicide than white Americans. Almost half—47.3 percent—of all offenders were under the age of 25, with one in 10 offenders under the age of 18. While television and films consistently portray women in jeopardy from murder, men make up nearly 75 percent of all homicide victims. Women, however, are the main victims of sex-related homicides (80 percent).

When homicide occurs to the most vulnerable in society, it tends to stir people's emotions. **Infanticide** is the murder of children under the age of five, while **eldercide** is the murder of persons 65 and older. Infanticide is the only category of homicide that increased during the 1990s, although it did decline slightly toward the end of the decade. Approximately 600 children under five years of age were killed in 2000, over half by a parent. Eldercide accounted for about 5 percent of all homicides in 2000. The rate of homicide of persons over 65 years of age has been declining since the early 1980s.

Q & A

Question: Who is most likely to want to murder me—someone I know or a stranger?

Answer: After examining Department of Justice statistics from 1976 to 2002, researchers found that 13.9 percent of murderers were strangers to their victims. In 6.9 percent of the cases, the murderer was the victim's spouse—a husband or wife. An additional 7.8 percent of murders were committed by some other family member, while 4.4 percent were committed by a boyfriend or girlfriend. Acquaintances were responsible for 32.6 percent of the murders studied. This classification includes friends, coworkers, fellow students, and people met at parties or events. The "acquaintance" tag is rather vague—it can also refer to drug dealers and their customers and even cover the relationship between a cab driver and a passenger. In 34.4 percent of the murders, the relationship between the victim and the murderer remained undetermined.

REASONS PEOPLE KILL

Among the facts and figures presented in the *2003 Statistical Abstract of the United States* is a listing of circumstances for murders that occurred the previous year. A good proportion of homicides—16.8 percent—were connected with crimes: 7.7 percent involved robbery, 4.1 percent involved drugs, and 0.5 percent involved sex offenses. The largest single cause for murder was disagreements. Disputes, whether over property, money, romance, or other reasons, accounted for 29.9 percent of killings. Other motives were cited in 19.4 percent of the cases, while the circumstances for 24.8 percent of murders are unknown.

Facts and figures seem inadequate in explaining *why* people commit homicide. In 1999, two students at Columbine High School in Colorado killed 13 people and then themselves. Responding to the murders, the American Psychological Association and MTV developed a program on school violence called Warning Signs. The program materials point to a number of reasons for the rise in violence and murder:

- Easy availability of guns. The United States has some of the weakest gun laws in the world. Although events like the Columbine massacre have occurred in other countries, only in the United States are large numbers of weapons so easily available.

■ Online availability of information on explosives. Before the Internet, such information was difficult to obtain, even in libraries. Today, that information is available with the click of a mouse.

■ The breakdown of the nuclear family. The increasing divorce rate and the blending of families seem to make it harder for children to find role models that can help them learn how to resolve conflicts. Children learn from what they see, not what they hear.

■ Violence on television and in movies. How many murders does the average person witness each week? The average TV watcher sees several during the course of a week. While violence may add excitement to television and movies, it also presents behaviors that some young people try to imitate.

■ The absence of a moral compass. In the past, young people had access to religious groups and organizations like the Boys Scouts and Girl Scouts that provided moral guidance. Today far fewer young people are exposed to these influences.

■ Both parents working. Many families need the income from the work of both parents. However, when both parents work, children have far more unsupervised time than was true for past generations. Most children do not build bombs in the basement, but decreased parental involvement offers the opportunity.

■ The breakdown of neighborhoods and communities. At one time, people tended to know everyone who lived on their block and many participated in community activities. Today families tend to spend more time apart from their community. Teenagers who do not feel connected to the community are more likely to act out in destructive ways.

■ The tendency of teens to form cliques. Teen movies have turned the social structure in high schools—jocks and popular kids on top, others on the fringe—into a stereotype. Unfortunately, the stereotype has some basis in fact. Conflicts among groups within a school have always existed, but today they are more violent, often involving weapons instead of fists.

■ Healthy teen rebellion getting out of hand. Teenagers struggle to become their own person, in part by rebelling against their parents. However, this normal process can go too far. If rebellion cuts all lines of communication between parents and teens, everyone suffers.

Homicides have decreased with the general decline of crime rates in recent years. However, 1999 statistics compiled by the Centers for Disease Control and Prevention on the top 10 causes of death for Americans still point out some disturbing facts. In the 10- to 14-year-old age range, homicide was third on the list. For the 15- to 19-year-old group, homicide was the second-highest cause of death.

See also: Gang Violence; Media and Violence; School Violence; Teens and Violence; Weapons of Violence

FURTHER READING
Ewing, Charles Patrick. *When Kids Kill.* New York: HarperCollins, 1995.

■ LEGAL INTERVENTIONS

The involvement of the law—usually by the actions of law enforcement agents—in the course of arresting or attempting to arrest lawbreakers, suppress disturbances, maintain order, or other legal actions.

The 2001 annual report of the Department of Justice (DOJ) found that 441,000 people serve as local police officers, with 200,000 additional officers serving at the state level. Federal agencies have another 93,000 people with the authority to make arrests. Including the courts and prison systems, the Bureau of Justice Statistics reported that some 2.3 million people worked in the criminal justice system in 2001. That represented an 81 percent rise in manpower since 1982.

What do all those law enforcement people do? Traditionally, police worked to deter crime by patrolling the streets (usually in police cars)

and apprehending offenders. Since the late 1960s, the police in many communities have been emphasizing crime prevention through **community policing.** Community policing is a partnership between police and the citizens of a community to prevent crime. Responsibility for reducing crime is placed on local police commanders who work with residents to identify threats to the community.

A 1995 National Institute of Justice report discusses some community policing strategies. Departments set up neighborhood-based offices or stations and designate "community" or "neighborhood" officers. Foot patrols are used to help an officer get to know the neighborhood and its residents even as the officer's presence discourages criminal activity. Some police departments also use bicycle patrols and involve residents in local community patrols and citizen police academies.

Police agencies that responded to the 1995 DOJ report listed a number of benefits of community policing. These benefits included a physical improvement in neighborhoods and more positive attitudes toward the police among residents. Police officers or deputies felt greater satisfaction with their job and the crime rate in localities using community policing dropped.

How does the typical police officer see his or her job? In a 1995 article in the *City Journal,* George L. Kelling, a social scientist specializing in police matters, discussed an internal survey of the New York Police Department. Kelling found that 91 percent of the officers believed that the public had little understanding of police problems. In addition, 75 percent disagreed with the statement that police officers and the public had a good relationship, while 81 percent agreed with the statement that the public believed police used too much force.

Kelling also offered an interesting view of the problems of policing from an officer's point of view. Seeing a heated argument between a cab driver and passenger, an officer has three hypothetical responses. By intervening before things get violent, the officer keeps the peace but gets no official recognition. By waiting until the argument escalates, the officer could make an arrest and receive official credit. If, however, the officer intervenes and something goes wrong, the result could be a complaint that affects the officer's future career.

POLICE ABUSE

One of the biggest challenges for police in the United States is building and maintaining positive relationships with their community. The vast majority of police officers are positive role models in their communities, enforcing the law fairly and justly. However, since the beginning of law enforcement efforts more than 200 years ago, there have been conflicts between officers and citizens. A notable example took place in 1999. In February, Amadou Diallo, a Nigerian immigrant, was killed by New York City police officers who fired 41 shots at the unarmed man. That June, Chicago police shot and killed two African Americans, LaTanya Haggerty and Robert Russ, at two traffic stops, six hours apart. Perhaps the best-known case took place in 1991. After a car chase, Los Angeles police officers repeatedly struck Rodney King with a nightstick. The beating changed the way many citizens viewed police behavior, in part because the incident was videotaped. The video was shown nationwide for weeks and triggered riots in Los Angeles that resulted in a billion dollars' worth of damage.

Fact Or Fiction?

The police come down hard on people depending on their race or where they come from.

Fact: A 2002 study in the journal *Criminology* covered 3,000 police encounters in two cities. Rather than race, citizen behavior was the most significant factor in triggering disrespectful policing. People with low self-control, males, young people, and those with low-income levels tended to receive more disrespect from police. The study found that people from minority groups actually showed less disrespect for the police than whites. However, the study also revealed that police did display a cultural bias against those they perceived to be on the social and economic fringes of society.

In 1996, just five years after the Rodney King case, another video of Los Angeles police officers beating an immigrant man and woman after a lengthy car chase received national attention. In 2000 a series of abuses in Los Angeles once again brought the practices of the LAPD to the nation's attention.

In a 2002 article in the *Journal of Criminal Justice*, incidents of police misconduct were related to public opinion. The most significant drops in approval ratings followed the Rodney King video. The number of people expressing confidence in the police dropped by 43 percent in the white community, 49 percent in the Hispanic community and by 50 percent in the black community. On a positive note, all drops in confidence were eventually erased and levels of confidence returned to normal with the passage of time after each incident.

More than 75 percent of minority residents felt the behavior described above was not an exception but regular behavior by officers on the force. Research reported in a 2000 issue of the *Journal of Criminal Justice* points out that citizen complaints are most commonly related to how well the people in the police match the people in the community. Age also becomes a factor. Police departments with older officers tend, on average, to have more citizen complaints made against them.

Residents were so outraged by the treatment they were receiving from the police that the Los Angeles Police Department (LAPD) made significant changes in its procedures to address the problem. The city appointed a new police chief, who made efforts to hire officers from various ethnic backgrounds so that the profile of the police force more closely matched the profile in the community. The city also set up a civilian review board, a group of citizens to deal with cases of possible police misconduct. Although the new board addressed many community concerns regarding police behavior, it also faced many challenges, specifically resistance from officers over decisions being made by people outside the force. The city also set up an independent team of investigators to examine reports of poor behavior by the police. In the past, internal members of the police force would look into such charges.

Efforts such as those completed by the LAPD can be done in any community and within any police force. Each is an attempt to improve relationships between local residents and the police. When relationships are strong, citizens can play an active role actually assisting police in the battle to reduce violence in their neighborhoods.

CITIZEN DISRESPECT

While Los Angeles has received much attention for some of the challenges they have faced, the issue confronting most police departments is a lack of respect for police officers. People expect the police to protect them and their property. Unfortunately, when confronted by police, some people fight back or verbally abuse officers.

Civilians may have reasons for resisting the efforts of local officers. A 2003 article in the *Journal of Criminal Justice* points out that one major cause for resistance is a belief that the officer is acting unjustly. If many officers gather around a person, he or she may feel threatened, overwhelmed, and scared. If the police stop a driver in a high traffic location or many bystanders are watching, embarrassment may trigger some defiance of the police in an effort to save face or preserve social standing in the community. The feeling of having one's freedom restricted, real or perceived, may also trigger resistance. Not surprisingly however, the best predictor of whether individuals will resist police efforts is whether or not they were using alcohol or drugs at the time of arrest. These substances lower inhibitions, leaving people likely to act in ways they would not even consider when not under the influence of a drug.

A 2001 study on police use of force by the International Association of Police Chiefs found that between 1995 and 2000, 46 percent of the traffic stops in which police had to use force occurred when the subject was under the influence of alcohol or drugs. Intoxicated drivers were three times more likely to attempt force against police, most often using their automobiles, knives, or baseball bats.

Police work can be dangerous, and in some officers have engaged in misconduct. However, the overwhelming majority of police officers dedicate themselves to controlling violence and making sure citizens are safe.

Q & A

Question: How can I help local police make my community safer?

Answer: You might consider some of the community involvement programs run by police departments. D.A.R.E., or Drug Abuse Resistance Education, teams police officers and teachers to discuss drug problems and also involves parents. G.R.E.A.T., Gang Resistance Education And Training, is a joint outreach program of the Federal Bureau of Alcohol, Tobacco, and Firearms and local police departments to schools, students, and parents. The Law Enforcement Explorers offers a more hands-on experience with police work for 14-

to 20-year-olds. This program is a joint effort between police and the Boy Scouts. You can also discuss other community involvement programs such as Block Watch and citizen patrols with your family members. Inquire about any of these programs with your local police force. If the programs aren't available, you may be able to encourage local police to start some of them.

See also: Communities and Violence; Criminals and Violent Activity; Drugs and Violence; Social Costs of Violence

FURTHER READING
Asirvathan, Sandy. *Police and Policing.* Philadelphia, Pa.: Chelsea House Publishers, 2002.

■ MEDIA AND VIOLENCE

The means of communication that reach large numbers of people, including newspapers, magazines, radio, television, films, and electronic communication. In bringing information and entertainment to millions of Americans, the media also depict many acts of violence. In the news media, consumers encounter wars, terrorist attacks, and a variety of crimes. In the entertainment media, many of the adventure and suspense stories that people read, see on the screen, or interact with in computer games contain violence. Even the music industry has developed a cult of violence, with songs about crime, shootings, police confrontations, and the mistreatment of women.

Violence in the media is not new. The first black-and-white film was a cowboy movie about a train robbery. Both the outlaws and the sheriff's posse blazed away with their six-shooters, and people fell dead. What is different today is the nature of the violence. It is more graphic, more sexual, and more frequent. But does it inspire acts of violence?

HOW MUCH VIOLENCE IS THERE?

When it comes to television, the most comprehensive research on violence was released in 1998. Responding to a challenge from a U.S. senator, the cable television industry paid for a three-year study involving researchers from four universities. In each year, the researchers studied 2,700 programs from 2,000 hours of broadcasts on 20 channels. They found that 61 percent of the shows contained violent content and that very few shows established consequences for the perpetrators. According to the Nielsen Group, which rates TV-show viewership, children watch 20 or more hours of television per week on average. Based on that estimate, children see approximately 10,000 acts of violence every year, mostly by characters who show no feelings about their actions and who, for the most part, go unpunished.

As for music, a 1989 article in *Psychological Reports* counted 18 acts of aggression per hour in the music videos on MTV. Violent video games often boast huge body counts. In "Carmegeddon," a game cited in a 1999 article in *Time* magazine, players could run over as many as 330,000 people going through all the levels in the game. Imagine how many more acts of aggression we view today.

Q & A

Question: If I watch a murder mystery at the theater, am I just going to snap one day and recreate what I saw?

Answer: Acting violently comes from a combination of many factors, both personal and environmental. However, for some people the interaction with media violence can cause a problem. In the lead-up to the massacre at Columbine High School in 1999, one of the two gunmen put up a customized version of the shoot-'em-up game "Doom" on his Internet Web site. The game featured two shooters, and all of the people being shot were unable to fire back. The pair also made a videotape for a class project in which they roamed the school, shooting athletes. In this case, the relationship between fantasy, media, and actual commission of a crime yielded 13 murders and the suicides of the two young gunmen.

WHAT IS THE EFFECT?

While researchers have managed to count violent episodes in the media, they have not been as successful in measuring the impact of that violence—especially on young people. Some scientists have dismissed laboratory experiments that measure aggressive reactions to violence in the media as having no relation to real life. Even when researchers agree that violence does have an effect, they disagree as to what that effect may be.

A 2001 article in the *Journal of the American Academy of Child and Adolescent Psychiatry* summarized research in the field from the previous 10 years. According to the article, people who view many hours of violence on television are more likely to exhibit violence as a means of solving conflict than those who watch less TV. The younger children are, and the more violence they are exposed to, the more aggressive their behavior and their scores on psychological tests.

Most of the research also identifies yet another issue, the desensitization of individuals to violent acts. In other words, the more violence a person is exposed to, the less likely that person is to be shocked, appalled, or angry about violence in his or her neighborhood. People who see violence come to accept it and are less likely to try to reduce violence.

In her book *The Loss of the Assumptive World,* grief therapist Linda Goldman discussed the impact of media on the way young people see the future. The "assumptive world" is a reflection of what kids take for granted: safety, love, trust, self-worth. As children view more and more violence, it erodes their idea of how safe they, or the world around them, may be. Goldman noted that children who survive terrible events feel unsafe, less valued, and more vulnerable. She believes that children who see no future for themselves experience hopelessness and fear. They are also more likely to turn to negative behaviors.

In the 2001 *Report from the Surgeon General on Youth Violence,* the country's highest-ranking public health officer discussed the impact of violence in the media. Electronic media can be found in almost every household and young Americans spend more than four hours a day with television, computers, VCRs and DVDs, and a variety of video games. Psychologists currently believe that some of the new interactive media may influence children's behavior even more powerfully than earlier products. In other words, the act of killing someone in a video game may make more of an impression than passively watching a killing on a TV screen.

Testing such beliefs, however, will not be possible until psychologists and other social scientists develop more accurate ways of measuring exposure to violence and how the patterns of that exposure vary depending on age, gender, and other distinctions.

A DISTORTED IMAGE

When violence in movies and television becomes part of the political debate in the United States, the focus is almost always on its impact on children. In his 2003 book *The 11 Myths of Media Violence*, media professor W. James Potter argued that the emphasis on young people is misguided. Exposure to violence affects all ages, all ethnicities, and both genders. By focusing on just one group, he maintains, the nation will not resolve the larger issue. Managing the amount of violence to which people of all ages are exposed is a better approach.

One of the myths that Potter addresses is the common belief that media violence is merely a reflection of violence in society. Potter used the research on the National Television Violence Study, which reviewed programming 17 hours each day on 23 channels and found approximately 18,000 acts of violence every three weeks, the equivalent of 936,000 acts of violence per year. Considering the fact that there are many more channels than the ones monitored, and seven more hours to the day, Potter estimated that television shows about 2.5 million violent acts each year. Using government crime statistics, he found that 1.4 million violent offenses were actually committed in the United States during the previous year. Is television a reflection of the real world? Potter says it is not. In his opinion, television grossly overestimates the degree of violence in Americans society.

A study described in a 2003 article in the *Journal of Criminal Justice and Popular Culture* monitored the crimes portrayed in the three highest-rated criminal justice dramas. Murder or attempted murder made up 66 percent of the offenses, with property crimes like theft or fraud making up only 9 percent of these prime-time crimes. Consulting the Federal Bureau of Investigation's Uniform Crime Reports for the same year, researchers found that in New York (the setting for two of the programs), most of the crimes were against property, with violent crime making up only 26.4 percent of the total and murder less than 1 percent. In Boston, the locale of the other show, violent crimes made up only 21 percent of crime total, with murder coming in at 0.4 percent.

Admittedly, a murder probably makes for a more suspenseful episode than a car theft. A sensational murder will also capture more news attention than an interfaith gathering to pray for peace. These choices, however, do not reflect reality. They serve more as advertisements for a violent, hostile world "out there"—and motivate some people to react more aggressively than the real world needs.

Fact Or Fiction?

One person can do very little about violence on TV.

Fact: Dealing with violence on television may need the work of many people, but it can begin with one person. A good starting point is to examine the way you watch TV. Another is by learning how to examine and criticize programs. Acquiring media literacy skills is an important step in controlling TV rather than having TV control you.

Read and research the problems associated with TV violence. What are the financial and organizational reasons for violent shows and films? Look for ways to bring up the problem in schoolwork, such as essays or reports. Discuss this issue with your teachers and with local TV stations. Most stations these days have Web sites. Why not contact them and express your concerns?

You might even help to bring your school and a local TV station together on a project, like videotaping public service announcements about violence. There's a lot to be done—and a lot one person can do to make a difference.

See also: Communities and Violence; Criminals and Violent Activity; Gang Violence; School Violence; Violent Behavior, Causes of

FURTHER READING
Edgar, Kathleen J. *Everything You Need to Know about Media Violence.* New York: Rosen Publishing Group, 1998.

■ RAPE
See: Sexual Violence

■ REHABILITATION AND TREATMENT OF PERPETRATORS
Efforts to help those convicted of crimes return to and function effectively in society. Originally, prison sentences were intended solely as punishments. However, officials in the correctional system

have long believed that one of their missions is to rehabilitate offenders.

Conviction for a particularly violent or other serious crime can put a person in prison for life. However, the overwhelming majority of prisoners serve shorter terms. If, upon release, they can become productive citizens, not only they but also society benefits.

Some former prisoners return to criminal behaviors. Repeating or returning to criminal behavior is called **recidivism.** Corrections experts measure recidivism rates to determine the success or failure of rehabilitation efforts.

INFLUENCES ON RECIDIVISM

In 2002, the Bureau of Justice Statistics released the results of a study of 272,111 former prisoners over a three-year period after their release. That number represented about two-thirds of the prisoners released from state prisons that year. The bureau requested records from 15 states with large and diverse populations. Of the released prisoners, 60 percent were rearrested and 40 percent were reconvicted within three years of leaving prison. The Kentucky Corrections Division has reported similar numbers: 40 percent of violent offenders were back in jail within one year of release. The division also reported that 33 percent of weapons violators and 14 percent of sex offenders were also back in prison within a year of release. Offenders do not necessarily return to prison for the same crime that resulted in their earlier conviction. Many were sent back for technical violations such as using alcohol or drugs, failing to report for curfews, or not attending treatment meetings.

While people commonly believe crime involves large amounts of money, studies contradict this notion. A 2000 article in *Criminology* suggests that crime is a lot of work, with street criminals engaging in robbery, burglary, and theft, auto theft, con games, forgery, and drug dealing. While some criminals take in thousands of dollars a month, 50 percent would be described as low-earning, and 63 percent would be described as inefficient, having to commit a large number of crimes, which increases the chances of arrest. A 2003 study in the *American Journal of Sociology* found criminals "earning" thousands of dollars a month but also losing money to expensive drug addictions and from being incarcerated. Released inmates with a criminal record often face difficulty in getting jobs. Also, a 2003 research paper for the Urban Institute's roundtable on prisoner reentry to society and work found a 30 to 50 percent unemployment rate among newly released prisoners, and an earnings rate of only $250–$500 a month.

Psychological problems may also affect a released inmate's chances of being sent back to prison. A 2002 study in the *Journal of Interpersonal Violence* of previously convicted adolescents found that those who had difficulty in controlling their behaviors, especially impulsive behavior, often were arrested again. A 2001 study reported in the *International Journal of Offender Therapy and Comparative Criminology* followed 480 graduates, ages 15 to 40, of a correctional "boot camp" (a prison that uses military-style training) for three years. Researchers found that the earlier in life individuals commit violent offenses, the more difficulty they have fitting into society and the more likely they are to commit crimes as they grow older.

A number of programs try to help rehabilitate those who have been convicted of violent crimes. Many prisons have treatment programs for inmates. After their release, many former prisoners participate in parole and community service.

TREATMENT PROGRAMS IN DETENTION AND PRISON

After an individual's conviction for a crime, he or she is sentenced to prison. That sentence can offer that individual an opportunity to change. Prison authorities try to encourage and guide that change through prison-based treatment programs. A wide variety of approaches have been tried over the years, but research has indicated which are most effective. A 2001 study on European methods published in *Psychology in Spain* and a 2002 study by American researchers in *Behavior Science and the Law* reached similar conclusions. Programs that teach inmates how to control their behavior and improve their attitudes prove the most effective in reducing recidivism.

Behavior modification is a form of treatment that uses psychological tools such as positive and negative reinforcement (rewards and punishments) to promote changes in behavior. Prison behavior modification programs try to teach appropriate responses to conflict. Instead of getting angry and punching someone, offenders learn to react more appropriately.

One system of positive reinforcement is based on a **token economy,** an arrangement in which those who act in an appropriate way receive tokens that can be used to purchase desirable items. This system works best in controlled environments. A token to get a snack has

National Rate of Recidivism, Within Three Years, of State Prisoners Released in 1994, by Prisoner Characteristics

Prisoner characteristics	Percent of all released prisoners	Rearrested	Reconvicted	Returned to prison with a new prison sentence	Returned to prison with or without a new prison sentence
All released prisoners	100	67.5	46.9	25.4	51.8
Gender					
Male	91.3	68.4	47.6	26.2	53.0
Female	8.7	57.6	39.9	17.3	39.4
Race					
White	50.4	62.7	43.3	22.6	49.9
Black	48.5	72.9	51.1	28.5	54.2
Other	1.1	55.2	34.2	13.3	49.5
Ethnicity					
Hispanic	24.5	64.6	43.9	24.7	51.9
Non-Hispanic	75.5	71.4	50.7	26.8	57.3
Age at release					
17 or younger	0.3	82.1	55.7	38.6	56.6
18–24	21.0	75.4	52.0	30.2	52.0
25–29	22.8	70.5	50.1	26.9	52.5
30–34	22.7	68.8	48.8	25.9	54.8
35–39	16.2	66.2	46.3	24.0	52.0
40–44	9.4	58.4	38.0	18.3	50.0
45 or older	7.6	45.3	29.7	16.9	40.9
Number of released prisoners with information	272,111	272,111	260,226	254,720	227,788

Source: Bureau of Justice Statistics, 2002.

little value when one can walk to the nearest convenience store and buy snack foods. It becomes more desirable in a setting in which one is not free to move about. Prison is the ultimate controlled environment, where token economies have been at work since the 1970s. The technique is considered especially useful in dealing with young offenders. A 2002 report, *What Works in Reducing Young People's Involvement in Crime*, by the Australian Institute of Criminology, confirms this system's usefulness.

Cognitive–behavioral treatment is a form of therapy that helps people understand and control the thoughts and emotions that cause various behaviors. In prison-based programs, inmates usually work in groups rather than individually to learn positive social skills. They learn to solve problems instead of acting aggressively, positive reasoning instead of hair-trigger reactions, and thoughtful responses instead of aggressive behavior. Prisoners can acquire many different strategies for dealing with conflict in a positive fashion rather than resorting to violence as a solution.

Cognitive-behavioral therapy concentrates on a series of mental steps—thoughts and emotions—that occur in the brain before taking an action. By breaking the **cycle of events,** as it is called, professionals can help inmates keep an action from taking place. The process is called **relapse prevention.** In a 2000 article in *Behavioral Science and the Law,* describing a relapse-prevention program for violent sex offenders, the author points out that no single event triggers relapses to violent behavior. The crime proceeds from a series of emotions, fantasies, and thoughts to a plan not only for an attack but also to remove inhibitions against committing the attack. By the time a person has stifled the feeling that "I shouldn't be doing this," nothing will stop the resulting violence. Cutting off the thought and emotional process earlier can prevent the criminal act. The goal is for offenders to learn to take responsibility for their actions, recognize when they are moving toward violent behavior, and to control the impulse.

PAROLE AND COMMUNITY SERVICE

Parole is an agreement between a prisoner and prison authorities. The prison agrees to release the prisoner as long as he or she agrees to be supervised and follow a set of rules or conditions. The purpose of these conditions is to keep the released prisoner from returning to prison. The Texas Youth Commission, for example, has established programs for young offenders that include education, therapy while in the correctional system, work programs, and training designed to increase self-discipline. The Texas program has reduced recidivism for youth who participate in the program compared to young prisoners who chose not to take part.

The Bureau of Justice Statistics reports that in 2000, 41 percent of prisoners nationwide successfully completed their parole and supervision. That rate has remained consistent since 1990.

Community service describes voluntary efforts to improve a community or neighborhood. Courts can impose community service in addition to a prison sentence or as an alternative to prison. Sometimes offenders are set to work menial tasks, such as cleaning up parks or roadsides. Often, however, community service involves helping victims of crimes similar to those the offender committed, or educating the public about the behavior that led to the offender's arrest. A 2000 report on the Ohio community service program appeared in *Corrections Management Quarterly.* The article stated that participants in the community service program had a recidivism rate of only 20 percent, compared to a 36 percent rate for the general prison population. In addition, the more hours of community service prisoners performed, the less likely they seem to be to commit new crimes.

TEENS SPEAK

I Didn't Realize How It Hurt

Jake is a freshman in a junior college. He volunteers in several local programs.

"I used to think the scariest thing I had ever had to deal with was standing in front of a judge and admitting I beat up my girlfriend—at least she used to be my girlfriend. That's over. We got into an argument over my looking at another girl, and I popped her—right as a cop came around the corner.

"I thought I got off pretty lightly in court, just a small fine and 250 hours of community service. Then I found out they'd assigned me to the local women's shelter. I worked at the front desk, helping to admit women and their children to a safe place where they could get away from abusive relationships."

Jake shudders. "At first, I almost wished they had put me away. Now I understand why they did it. What I saw at the shelter really scared me. Some women came in covered with blood; others were just so scared that all they could do was cry for hours. I saw one woman come in seeming just fine. She didn't look beat up, she wore nice clothes; you'd think she could be anyone's mom. For a while I couldn't figure out why she was there. Then her boyfriend turned up yelling. He began throwing chairs around, finally breaking a window. The guy was crazy."

He shrugs. "My community service is over now, but I go over to the Teen Center and talk with the guys there. I tell them that abuse lasts longer than the 10 seconds it takes to hit someone. It can stay with people for life. It's not the most comfortable thing, having people stare at you while you talk about your far-from-proudest moments. But I know a lot of these guys, and hopefully they can learn something to keep them from ending up where I did."

Rehabilitating people who have broken the law, especially violent offenders, is not a simple task, nor is it accomplished easily. If people can be saved from a life of crime, however, the task must be attempted—if only to avoid adding to the already crowded prison population in the United States.

See also: Criminals and Violent Activity; Sexual Violence; Violent Behavior, Causes of

FURTHER READING
Blue, Rose, and Corinne J. Nader. *Punishment and Rehabilitation.* Philadelphia, Pa.: Chelsea Press, 2001.

ROAD RAGE
Violence shown by drivers in traffic, often as a sign of stress. Practical demonstrations of road rage can be found on almost any major roadway. Imagine a beautiful, sunny day with you and your friends out

on a short cruise. The goal is to have fun and enjoy the day. Then, a car buzzes your front bumper while changing lanes, almost knocking you and your friends into a ditch. Or a woman who could easily be described as your grandmother is driving 45 miles per hour in the left lane of the highway. She refuses to move out of the lane to allow you to pass. How do you react?

Most people might express some annoyance or laugh it off. For too many drivers, however, the highway has become something like the Wild West, a place where any inconsiderate or clumsy driving requires revenge or punishment with hair-trigger aggression. According to a 2001 article in *Social Psychiatry and Psychiatric Epidemiology*, the term *road rage* did not exist until the media began using it in the 1980s. The researchers in the article found that over 50 percent of all drivers have experienced a road rage incident in the last five years.

DEGREES OF ROAD RAGE

A 1999 study in the *Chronicle of the American Driver and Traffic Safety Education Association* noted four degrees of road rage. The first degree involves a gesture or a few select words directed at the offending driver. In the second degree of rage, an exchange of gestures or cursing occurs between the parties involved. This exchange may escalate into expressions of anger that distract both drivers from surrounding traffic, increasing the chance of a crash.

As the level of aggression builds to the third degree, drivers begin harassing actions such as flashing high beams, impeding the progress of other vehicles or, when being tailgated, stopping quickly to frighten other drivers. Reaching the fourth and greatest degree of rage, drivers become still more aggressive, having verbal or physical confrontations with the people who offended them, causing injury. Drivers may also display weapons as threats while cursing people who are driving too slowly. In some situations, the weapons even get used. Researchers view this fourth degree as the most dangerous scenario—one that has occurred with increasing frequency over the past 10 years.

In 1997 testimony before Congress, the administrator of the National Highway Traffic Safety Administration reported that aggressive driving contributed to one-third of automobile crashes nationwide in the previous year—and two-thirds of the 41,907 crash-related deaths.

No clear-cut, single reason can explain why people allow their anger to control how they drive. However, researchers have developed a few explanations.

SELF-DETERMINATION THEORY

In 2001, researchers at the University of Houston used what they called the self-determination theory to explain aggressive behavior on the road. This theory is based on the idea that free will can be used to understand people's motivations and personalities and tries to categorize people into two personality types. Autonomy-oriented types believe that they determine their own responses and actions. Control-oriented types are more likely to attribute their behaviors to the actions of others. To put the difference simply, the first type represents students who do homework because they see a benefit in doing well in class or earning good test scores, or they enjoy learning something new. The second type would include students who do their homework only because their parents make them to it.

Autonomy-oriented people generally have a more positive self-esteem, are more likely to take responsibility for their actions, and are less likely to become angry when provoked. Control-oriented people are more likely to react based on the pressures of the world around them and attribute their behavior to those forces rather than to their own actions.

How does this theory relate to driving? The University of Houston researchers found that control-oriented drivers showed more aggression on the road and were more likely to show anger, get into accidents, and receive tickets for poor driving. They also reacted more aggressively to hostile gestures, slow or rude drivers, traffic delays due to road construction, and the presence of police.

A 2001 study published in the *Social Science Journal* found that although many drivers responded with road rage when traffic slowed, reckless driving by others was more likely to initiate a confrontation. The researchers discovered that differences in age or gender did not change their findings. Drivers decided whether to retaliate solely based on how angry they were about the triggering incident.

THE VIEW FROM BEHIND THE WHEEL

If you drive, you probably know whether you get angry while you are on the road. If you do, you must consider the possible consequences of your actions. Aggressive drivers get more tickets, become involved in more accidents, and place those in their vehicles at greater risk. In the long run, consequences may include higher insurance costs and the possibility of hurting another person—possibly someone you care for. The way you react is not controlled by the actions of others. If you get cut off in traffic, you may be annoyed, but it is not a personal attack.

Experts suggest that you slow down if you are angry. Speed plays a significant role in crashes. You can choose the driving speed for your car, regardless of the way others might be driving. Imagine you need to drive across town. It's a 10-mile drive and the speed limit is 45 miles per hour. Driving at the speed limit, you will arrive in a little over 13 minutes. If you decide you are in a hurry and take off at 55 miles per hour, you will arrive in just under 11 minutes. How important is that two minutes, especially when driving 10 miles over the speed limit increases your changes for a ticket, or a crash in which you and others may be injured?

If you find that you have a tendency toward road rage, practice stress management. When you feel yourself getting angry, take deep breaths, count to 10, play music you enjoy, whatever it takes to stay calm. In the long run, you win, because if you can learn to manage your emotions when you drive, you can use those skills in other aspects of your life as well.

Drivers have complained about increasing aggressiveness on the nation's highways for years. Uncontrolled road rage can lead to dangerous situations not only for the targets of angry motorists but also for the innocent drivers around them. People get into plenty of trouble by swinging baseball bats or pipes at people who provoke them. Turning a ton and a half of glass and metal—one's car—into a weapon can have serious, even fatal, consequences.

See also: Fight or Flight Response; Violent Behavior, Causes of

FURTHER READING
Winters, Adam. *Everything You Need to Know about Being a Teen Driver.* New York: Rosen Publishing Group, 2000.

■ ROBBERY
See: Social Costs of Violence

■ SCHOOL VIOLENCE

Any behavior that violates a school's educational mission, spoils a climate of respect, or jeopardizes the intent of the school to be free of aggression against persons or property, drugs, weapons, disruptions, and disorder. Based on this definition provided by the Center for the Prevention of School Violence and one offered by the Federal Bureau of Investigation (FBI), school violence can include anything from bullying to homicide.

THE SCOPE OF THE PROBLEM

Throughout the 1990s, school violence was associated with a series of sensational news headlines. In 1995, a 17-year-old in Giles County, Tennessee, brought a .22 rifle into his school, killing a teacher and a classmate. In Paducah, Kentucky, in 1997, a 14-year-old brought a pistol, two rifles, two shotguns, and 700 rounds of ammunition to school. Three girls died, and five other students were wounded. In 1998, an 11-year-old and a 13-year-old set themselves up as snipers outside their middle school in Jonesboro, Arkansas. After setting off a fire alarm, they opened fire as schoolmates filed into the parking lot. Four students and a teacher died.

In 1999, the most sensational incident to date took place. Two boys, 17 and 18 years old, brought guns and bombs into Columbine High School in Littleton, Colorado. They killed 12 students and one teacher and took their own lives. In 2005, a 16-year-old shot and killed nine people, including his grandfather and students and teachers at a high school in Red Lake, Minnesota.

A 2000 Secret Service report summarized 37 school attacks since 1974, attacks which left 54 dead and 124 wounded. Described as "an epidemic of school violence," these incidents triggered an avalanche of research, policy statements, and programs to address the issue of violence within the school setting.

The Centers for Disease Control and Prevention (CDC) collects information from teens across the nation by asking a series of questions. This annual study, the Youth Risk Behavior Surveillance System (YRBSS), revealed the following in 2001:

- More than 400,000 youths ages 10 to 19 were injured as a result of violence in the year 2000. Approximately one in 28 of these injuries required hospitalization.

- In a survey of high school students, more than one-third of respondents reported being in a physical fight in the previous 12 months. Of those, 4 percent were injured seriously enough to require medical treatment by a doctor or nurse.

- Most young homicide victims are killed with guns. In 1999, 82 percent of homicide victims 15 to 19 years old were killed with firearms.

- About 6 percent of students carried a weapon such as a gun, knife, or club on school property within the month before the survey.

- More than 6 percent of students did not go to school on one or more of the past 30 days because they felt unsafe at school or on their way to or from school.

- Nearly 9 percent of students had been threatened or injured with a weapon on school property one or more times during the past 12 months.

THE CONTAGIOUS NATURE OF SCHOOL VIOLENCE

When people describe the increase of school violence as an "epidemic," they do not refer to a disease carried by germs but a phenomenon that spreads through psychological means. Although personal decisions play a part, participants in a 1998 Department of Justice research forum pointed out that violence can become "contagious." Violence can reach epidemic proportions when young people decide to carry weapons and act more aggressively, causing others around them to do the same.

The media can also play a major part in spreading the infection. Researchers became aware of this effect decades ago. A 1986 article in the *New England Journal of Medicine* linked media coverage of suicides with sudden surges in teen suicide rates. A similar connection exists between media coverage and school rampages. In the weeks after the exhaustively covered tragedy at Columbine High School, every state except Vermont reported threats of similar actions. Would-be copycats were discovered planning gun attacks or bombings in high schools and middle schools as far from Littleton, Colorado, as California and Florida.

In 2001, a pair of high school boys in Kansas were caught before they attempted an imitation of the Columbine massacre. That same year, officials were unable to stop a 15-year-old boy in Santee, California. His attack resulted in the murder of two students and the wounding of 13 others.

Admittedly, screaming headlines and top story status on newscasts help to focus attention on a problem. The saying in newsrooms across the country is short and brutal—"If it bleeds, it leads." In the case of school violence, however, such coverage also serves to promote additional violence, in the opinion of some media observers.

FEAR OF CLASSMATES

In his book *School Violence,* Jeff Jones quotes President Bill Clinton as saying, "In most schools it's not the sensational acts of violence, but the smaller acts of aggression, threats, scuffles, and constant back talk that take a terrible toll on the atmosphere of learning, on the morals of the teachers, on the attitudes of students."

Fear is the enemy of education. Students and teachers are unable to concentrate if they are continually looking over their shoulders. Unfortunately, at too many schools in the United States, that is exactly what they are doing.

In 2003, the Departments of Justice and Education issued a joint report, "Indicators of School Crime and Safety." Among the many facts and figures in the report was a statistic on the percentage of students between the ages of 12 to 18 who feared an attack at school or on the way to or from school. In 1995, that figure stood at 12 percent of students. In 1999, the figure dropped to 7 percent, and in 2001, to 6 percent.

Students also reported whether they avoided one or more places in school. In 1995, 9 percent admitted to staying away from certain spots at school. In 1999, the figure had dropped to 5 percent, and it stayed the same in 2001.

The Department of Education's 1995 National Condition of Education Survey showed that students had good reason to be fearful. Almost 41 percent of high school seniors reported having property stolen, while 26 percent reported having their property deliberately damaged. About 16 percent reported being injured, with nearly 5 percent of students harmed by weapons. That same year, Louis Harris and Associates took a poll of students. The firm found that many students made serious changes in their lives because of violence. About 22 percent changed friends, 13 percent the way they traveled to or from school, and 10 percent gave up a particular activity or sport. Perhaps the most telling response, however, was the 12 percent who believe their grades suffered because of violence or the fear of violence.

Even if the improving trend in school safety cut these percentages in half, it would still mean that one in 20 American students fear places and people in their schools.

TEENS SPEAK

A Deadly Lesson

Steve is a high school senior and the quarterback on his school's football team.

Steve recalls Brian, a fellow student. "'Brian Brain-dead,' we used to call him—that, or 'Stick-boy' because he was so skinny. Those were the nicer names we used, ever since he transferred to our school last year. Brian never objected to the names or the pranks people pulled on him. Either that, or he quickly learned not to.

"I suppose we shouldn't have been surprised at his interest in school shootings. Everybody knew that would be his report for Contemporary Studies. I should have said something when one of the guys on the team tore up Brian's charts. But it was Brian Brain-dead, so who cared? Ralph was a linebacker—he could have broken Stick-boy over one knee."

Steve shakes his head. "Brian went home during lunch. I thought he was getting replacement charts. Instead, he came back with his dad's gun.

When he walked to the front of the class and shot out the window, I thought, 'I'm dead.' I mean, I was everything he hated—one of the popular kids, an athlete on the football team.

Then we heard the sirens in the distance. From the look on his face, Brian suddenly realized that being locked up in Juvie would be 10 times worse than school. So he used the gun—on himself."

Steve shuts his eyes. "Afterward, the news people were all over us. They wanted to know what movies Brian watched, what computer games he played—what they could blame. Nobody wanted to listen when we said we were all to blame. When I saw that gun, I kept thinking, 'I'm getting just what I deserve.' Too bad there's no way I can make it up to Brian."

SCHOOL-BASED PREVENTION STRATEGIES

Educators across the nation recognize the destructive nature of violence on the school environment. As a result, administrators have increased their efforts to keep the school environment positive and learning-oriented. Some schools have assigned staff or volunteers to monitor bathrooms and hallways and routinely check bags, desks, or lockers. Other administrators have brought uniformed police officers into their schools and utilized metal detectors and surveillance cameras. These efforts are aimed at making the school environment safer and less violent so that students can focus on schoolwork rather than their safety.

Many schools have also established programs to teach students how to avoid violent situations and to keep conflicts from becoming violent. The following sections examine some of these initiatives.

Self-control

One of the core concepts behind any attempt to curb school violence involves teaching young people to manage or regulate their emotions. When people feel angry, they do not automatically have to act on that emotion. They can instead work through their problems instead of turning to violence. Unfortunately, many young people have been exposed to so much anger and violence that they have never developed the ability to control their emotions.

In 2000, researchers from the University of Southern California examined how exposure to violence may affect the way people manage emotions. Their findings suggest that children who witness violent behavior are more likely to see violence as an acceptable response to conflict. Children who are victims of violence, not just witnesses, also have difficulty managing their emotions.

The Michigan Model for School Health Education identifies three steps to managing anger. First, individuals must identify what their triggers are. A **trigger** is an event that stimulates anger. When people know which events are most likely to make them angry, they can either avoid those situations or prepare themselves to deal with the tension. Knowing what is coming makes the situation less likely to get out of control.

Second, individuals need to recognize their anger. Anger is a natural emotion. People need to understand how their bodies respond to feelings of anger. How does the body respond to a trigger? How does the anger build?

The third step involves finding ways to cool the anger. Some people learn to remove themselves from environments that make them angry. The most effective approaches separate an individual from a conflict. Talking with someone about the problem can help, as can exercising or participating in an activity that one enjoys, like reading or even taking a nap.

Negotiation

Negotiation is a method of resolving conflict between two people—or groups—by conferring until a mutual agreement is reached. Suppose you lend money to a friend on several occasions. The amount is adding up, and you want him or her to pay you back. Your friend might respond, "I can't give you that much—I don't have it." By negotiating, you may be able to work out a system of repayments.

Sometimes people disagree on what is appropriate. By sitting down and discussing the issue, they may resolve the problem in such a way that everyone involved is satisfied with the result.

Mediation

One of the more popular approaches to curbing violence in schools is through **peer mediation,** a process by which a fellow student or member of the community helps resolve a conflict. A mediator is not just any student, however. He or she has received training in a six-step procedure:

1. Mediators explain that the arguing parties must reach their own agreement. In doing so, all sides need to respect one another, and allow one another to offer his or her case without interruptions.

2. Mediators ask each party to explain the problem and to express his or her feelings without becoming aggressive.

3. Each of the opposing parties is given time to state the problem.

4. Mediators restate and sum up the dispute based on what they heard and what they know about the problem. They may also ask questions to clarify the situation.

5. Mediators ask each side to come up with a solution for the problem and then restate their suggestions. Mediators do not offer their own solutions.

6. When both sides reach an agreement, they sign a contract that sets out what each party is willing to do.

A mediator's job is to look objectively at a conflict, not show favoritism, and come to an appropriate resolution.

Communication skills

Effective communication involves not only being able to say what one feels but also being able to hear what others have to say. Saying what one feels requires an ability to express oneself in a positive way. Describing what one is thinking or feeling without hurting someone else is a skill that does not come naturally to many people. It takes practice.

Situations in which people try to express why their feelings were hurt or how they have been offended are often tense. No one wants to say something that may end a friendship or start an argument. However, if one doesn't speak up, then acts that cause hurt feelings or cause offense will continue, which can cause even more damage to a friendship or relationship.

Communication requires not only speaking but also listening. Learning that one's words or actions have hurt someone's feelings can be difficult to hear. It is all too easy to be defensive. Then, while one plans how to respond to criticism, he or she stops listening. One cannot plan a counterattack and really listen to a complaint at the same time. The person who thinks ahead to how he or she should respond will probably miss the most important part of the discussion: *why* a friend is hurt or offended.

By keeping one's emotions in check and really paying attention to what a friend is saying, a person will have a much better understanding of the situation and will be able to come to a more effective solution to the conflict.

DID YOU KNOW?

Percentage of Schools Teaching Topics and Skills for Violence Prevention

	All schools	Elemen- tary schools	Middle/ junior high schools	Senior high schools
Topic				
Anger management	91.8	94.9	85.9	88.4
Bullying	91.2	96.3	88.0	72.6
Dating violence	62.2	N/A	52.2	82.7
Gun safety	45.7	54.3	33.6	27.4
Personal safety (e.g., dealing with strangers)	87.0	96.4	74.7	66.2
Pro-social behaviors	95.5	98.5	90.9	90.3
Sexual assault	60.5	N/A	52.3	77.4
Skill				
Communications skills to avoid violence	97.2	97.8	94.4	99.4
Decision-making skills to avoid violence	97.5	98.4	96.1	95.6
Goal-setting skills to avoid violence	91.5	95.1	84.0	88.8
Techniques to avoid interpersonal conflicts and fights	94.6	96.0	92.8	91.4

Source: Violence Prevention Fact Sheet, Centers for Disease Control and Prevention, 2000.

Programs to resolve conflict among students can play an important role in improving conditions in not only school but also their community. Those skills can make a positive difference in one's relationships. They can also help prevent school violence. While reports of school violence have decreased in recent years, the problem still remains a troubling one for too many students in the United States.

See also: Assault and Bullying; Criminals and Violent Activity; Media and Violence; Teens and Violence; Violent Behavior, Causes of

FURTHER READING
Orr, Tamra. *Violence in Our Schools.* New York: Franklin Watts, 2003.

■ SELF-MUTILATION
A deliberate but nonlethal injury to the body, including activities such as cutting or scratching oneself, burning, hitting oneself hard enough to bruise the skin or break a bone, or hair pulling. Even persistent nail-biting can be considered a low-level form of self-mutilation. The condition is also known as self-harm or self-injurious behavior. Whichever the name, it describes a serious and complicated disorder—one that is difficult to overcome.

WHY WOULD PEOPLE HURT THEMSELVES?
Pain is something everyone has to deal with. Athletes know the "agony of defeat"—especially the special pain of making a mistake on the playing field. Maybe someone just ended a relationship that he or she thought would last a lifetime. Talking to parents, teachers, or friends may help to relieve the pain. In time, most painful episodes pass and life moves on. Unfortunately, life does not move on for everyone, and for some the stress and guilt associated with a painful episode is turned inward. A small but growing percentage of people choose to inflict external physical damage on themselves as a way of coping with internal pain.

In his book *Living on the Razor's Edge,* family therapist Matthew Selekman discusses some of the factors that push young people into behaviors like "cutting." Cutting is just what it sounds like, using a razor or other sharp instrument to make cuts on the body. Selekman points out that the act of causing the injury is an attempt to relieve a significant emotional pain. It is also a sign that an adolescent needs assistance in working through an emotional crisis. Young people who practice this behavior may not have an underlying personality disorder and should not automatically be considered a victim of sexual abuse or someone with suicidal tendencies.

Psychologists and physicians have learned that causing bodily harm to oneself is usually a way of coping with feelings of unworthiness and a lack of connection to parents and other adult figures. What Selekman calls a **family breakdown** may cause some adolescents to feel as though their parents do not even know they exist. Feelings of unworthiness or abandonment are large burdens to carry, and adolescents who injure themselves are doing so to deflect some of their emotional pain. The key for these youths is to find out what is missing and try to rebuild that relationship.

A second reason for self-mutilation can be found in the pace of life today. Classes, organized sports, after-school jobs and activities can be stressful. The pressure to achieve academically and personally can be overwhelming. In the absence of a positive way of coping with such strains, some young people turn to self-injuring behaviors.

Third, Selekman points out that our society's demands for a quick resolution to problems may lead to incomplete treatment. Many young people who injure themselves are placed on medication, treating the symptom and hiding the fact that deeper emotion-based issues may be at the core of the problem rather than chemical imbalances in the brain.

In 2002, researchers for the American Psychological Association tried to identify ways of providing positive and negative reinforcement for young people who exhibit self-injuring behaviors. **Positive reinforcement** can be described as a reward or desirable result obtained from a behavior. It encourages repetition of an action. In contrast, **negative reinforcement** is a punishment or undesirable outcome obtained from a behavior. It discourages repetition. Most parents react with concern and attention when their children hurt themselves. Children who believe they are not noticed may learn that by hurting themselves, they receive the attention they desperately wish for.

Positive reinforcement may also come from peers, leading young people to take up or keep practicing the behavior. If friends think that cutting is cool, they may convince others to do so as well. If friends respond positively, giving people the attention they want, that reinforces the behavior.

Q & A

Question: How can I tell if one of my friends has a problem with self-mutilation?

Answer: It won't be easy, mainly because people try to hide this behavior as best as they can. However, scars or sores that your friend has explained away as cat scratches may be warning signs, especially if these injuries appear on the forearms.

Burn marks that appear to be caused by a cigarette or a flame may also be a sign of self-hurting. If your friend's explanation is brief, and he or she seems to be avoiding any discussion of his or her injuries, these too may be signs. None of these signs offer proof beyond a doubt. All of them can be caused by other things, and often are. If you know your friend is hurting emotionally, being aware of his or her pain and providing support may be a first step in helping him or her move away from self-injury.

TREATMENT OPTIONS

An important aspect in helping friends or family members to stop injuring themselves is to alter the way they think about themselves. Consider this common scenario: A mother expresses anger at her teenager, prompting thoughts such as "I'll never be good enough," and then self-abusive behavior begins. The place to intervene is at the middle step. It is impossible to control what a parent says or does, but one can control one's own responses to their words and actions. Individuals who cut or burn themselves feel poorly about themselves. Changing how one reacts to criticism and learning to recognize one's personal strengths can lead to a more positive result.

Because stress is such a significant factor in self-injury, learning techniques to manage stress can help. Exercise, meditation, keeping a journal, and many other techniques can help to improve one's outlook on life and move away from damaging behavior.

People struggling to stop self-injuring behaviors face a range of treatment options, depending on the amount of repetition and the severity of danger. In less severe cases, individuals may be able to find strategies for helping themselves by readings books on the subject. In more severe cases, medication, psychological therapy, or partial or inpatient hospitalization may be necessary.

Whatever form of treatment is needed, those who cut or engage in other forms of self-harm need help. Self-mutilation is an especially saddening form of violence because people direct it against themselves.

See also: Suicide

FURTHER READING
Winkler, Kathleen. *Cutting and Self-mutilation: When Teens Injure Themselves.* Berkeley Heights, N.J.: Enslow, 2002.

■ SEXUAL VIOLENCE
Physical act of aggression that includes a sexual act or sexual purpose. The World Health Organization (WHO) defines sexual violence in *The World Report on Violence and Health* as "a sexual act, an attempt to obtain a sexual act, unwanted sexual comments or advances, or acts to traffic a person's sexuality, using coercion, threats of harm or physical force, by any person regardless of relationship to the victim, in any setting, including but not limited to home and work."

Q & A

Question: Isn't rape an issue that only involves women?

Answer: Rape is an issue important to everyone in a society. Expressing violence through sexual acts is wrong. Furthermore, while women make up the large majority of rape victims, men are also victims. A 2001 article in *Human Rights Watch* points out the results of several surveys of inmates in U.S. correctional institutions. By a conservative estimate, one in 10 male prisoners is raped, sexually assaulted, or coerced into sexual contact by other inmates.

The victims include people of all ages and economic brackets—college students, young professionals, middle-aged people in wealthy suburbs, poor people in urban neighborhoods, even grandparents in nursing homes. Women, however, are overwhelmingly the targets of sexual violence. According to a Department of Justice report, the victims in 94 percent of completed rapes, 91 percent of attempted rapes, and 89 percent of both completed and attempted sexual assaults were women.

TEEN SPEAK

I Used to Be a Hero

Vince is large for his 17 years. He is presently suspended from his school's football team until a court hearing over accusations of rape.

"Not too long ago, people smiled when I walked by them in school. They cheered me on the football field, saying I would take the team to the state championships. That's all over now."

His shoulders hunch a little as he goes on. "A bunch of us were unwinding after a big game. Some beers, some music—a little company. I was with a cheerleader named Sherry—a really cute girl. We'd fooled around a little before . . . before what happened."

"This time, we really got into it, hot and heavy. And then she starts saying 'no.'"

Vince takes a deep breath. "Maybe if I hadn't been drinking—I don't know. I thought I could make her say 'yes.' Sherry was crying when I left.

"Nowadays when I walk down the halls in school, people look at me differently. And, of course, I'm off the team. College scouts were beginning to come around but not anymore."

He squeezes his eyes tightly shut. "All I ever wanted to do was play ball. But now, because I wanted somebody to say 'yes' instead of 'no,' I've sent my whole life down the tubes."

RAPE

The Federal Bureau of Investigation (FBI) runs the Uniform Crime Reporting service, which annually tabulates reports from law-enforcement agencies across the country. In 2002, according to those statistics, 95,136 forcible rapes were committed. However, not all rapes are reported. According to a Bureau of Justice Statistics report based on police and medical reports, only 36 percent of completed rapes, 34 percent of attempted rapes, and 26 percent of sexual assaults were reported to the police between 1992 and 2000. Another Bureau of Justice Statistics report, based on the National Crime Victims Survey, estimates that there were actually about 248,000 rapes, attempted rapes, and sexual assaults in 2001.

Who committed these offenses? When you hear the word *rape,* do you picture a stranger lurking in a dark alley? Or do you imagine a young man out on a date or a friend, even a relative? A 2002 report by the Department of Justice found that in 66 percent of sexual assault cases, the offender was someone the victim knew—a family member, a friend, or an acquaintance.

Defining rape

Forcible rape, as defined by the FBI's Uniform Crime Reporting system, is the carnal (sexual) knowledge of a female against her will.

Until the 1970s, U.S. laws defined rape as sexual penetration of a woman by a man who was not her husband, a crime under the English Common Law upon which American law is based. However, the Common Law was established through court cases dating back more than 700 years, much of it at a time when women were considered the property of their husbands who could force their wives to have sex if they desired. Common Law tended to protect men from accusations of rape rather than protecting women who suffered as a result of a rape.

Social changes, especially the rise of the feminist movement in the late 1960s, challenged this historical definition of rape. Increasingly, people in the United States and elsewhere viewed rape as a crime that has less to do with sex and more to do with violence and power.

Identifying possible rapists

In his book *Men Who Rape: The Psychology of the Offender,* A. Nicholas Groth, a clinical psychologist, identified four types of rapists. Federal and state law enforcement agencies use those categories to prevent rape and help capture perpetrators.

- The power-assertive rapist is usually aggressive, meeting his victims in settings like bars. He likes to control and degrade victims but does not intend to kill. His crimes are based on opportunity—he doesn't usually single out victims. Statistically, this type is responsible for approximately 40 percent of rapes.

- The power-reassurance rapist lacks the social skills to develop relationships with women and is often not athletic or aggressive. This type of rapist usually selects and stalks a victim. He may take trophies of his "conquests" or write about his activities in a diary. He often has a fantasy of a consensual relationship with a woman and is the least violent rapist. This type of rapist accounts for approximately 27.5 percent of rapes.

- The anger-retaliatory rapist feels hostile toward all women, has an explosive temper, and has little control over his impulses. He may also be a substance abuser. He does not single out a victim; his aggression is aimed at women in general. Attacks are usually spontaneous and brutal. Although he does not set out to kill victims, he may beat them to death if they resist or fail to escape. This type accounts for about 28 percent of rapes.

- The anger-excitation rapist enjoys torturing and killing victims for the thrill and sexual gratification of the acts. The person may select victims or take them in crimes of opportunity. This type of rapist is the most likely to kill and accounts for 4.5 percent of rapes.

Acquaintance rape

As the definition of rape has changed in society along with the legal interpretation, so has the image of the rapist. No longer is he seen as a stranger waiting in a dark corner. Today law enforcement officers and researchers recognize that a rapist could be a neighbor, a coworker, a friend of the family, a husband or boyfriend. A new term has evolved—**acquaintance rape**. It is a rape in which the victim knows the rapist. That category includes date rape—forced sex in which the perpetrator has an intimate or dating relationship with the victim.

Department of Justice statistics reveal that almost 70 percent of rape victims knew their assailant at the time of the incident. Although acquaintance rape is often portrayed as occurring on the first date, rape can occur at various stages of a relationship. Only one-third of date rapes take place on a first date. One of every four date rapes occurs after a couple has already dated a few times. Partners in long-term relationships commit an additional 30 percent of all acquaintance rapes.

Many Americans still believe a variety of myths about sexual relationships and rape. One myth is that a woman owes a man sex if he pays for the date. Another is that if a woman is sexually active, she does not really mean it when she say no; she's simply playing hard to get.

To avoid possible misunderstandings while dating, people must communicate about sexual behavior. Many men find it uncomfortable to bring up the subject, feeling it will "spoil the mood." Women may feel awkward saying something like, "I like you, and I'm having fun, but I do not intend to have sex tonight." However, a little embarrassment up front may save considerable trouble later.

Much of society still clings to these and other centuries-old myths, which place the blame on the victim. These myths about rape are not only untrue but may also be even illegal. In his book *Date Rape Prevention Book*, author Scott Lindquist points out a few these myths:

- Victims must struggle for an attack to count as rape.
- If the victim has had sex before, he or she cannot bring a charge of rape against the perpetrator.
- Victims themselves are to blame if they allow a risky situation to develop.
- Women who dress provocatively should expect to be raped.

These beliefs are based on old legal doctrines that made it almost impossible to charge a rapist, much less prove the offense. They attempt to shift the responsibility for the offender's behavior to the victim and away from the rapist. Nothing could be more wrong. No rationale can excuse forced sexual activity.

Rape crisis centers

At a time when society offered little support for rape victims, a number of women in the 1970s founded rape crisis centers in their communities.

Today most cities and towns have at least one such center. Many of them offer rape victims counseling and support groups. Victims also find advocates there willing to provide them with one-on-one support. For example, if a victim needs to go to a hospital for a medical examination, an advocate may accompany her to explain the procedures and provide assistance. If the victim decides to press charges against the rapist, advocates not only explain what to expect if the case goes to court but are often willing to stay with her throughout the trial. Advocates also provide help over the telephone on special lines open 24 hours a day, seven days a week. In addition, they try to keep the communities they serve informed about the problems associated with sexual assaults.

In a 1998 article in the *American Journal of Community Psychology* researchers reported on 168 rape crisis centers across the country. They found that those centers have expanded over the years to provide an ever-widening range of services for rape victims.

SEXUAL HARASSMENT

Sexual harassment is a form of sex discrimination that involves unwelcome sexual advances, requests for sexual favors, and other verbal or physical conduct of a sexual nature. Such harassment can create a hostile environment in the workplace or at school.

The law is vague in describing the specific acts that are considered harassment. In her book *Sexual Harassment, A Debate*, feminist philosopher Linda LeMoncheck points out that some forms of harassment are easily identified while others are based more on individual interpretation. One example is **sexual coercion,** the use of a supervisor's power to threaten an employee with being fired as a way of securing sexual favors. Sometimes, a supervisor may reward an employee who performs sexual acts with a promotion or a raise. This form of harassment is called **sexual bribery.** A supervisor who initiates physical contact—kissing, touching, pinching, or hugging—when that contact is not wanted is also easily identified as guilty of sexual harassment.

Sexual harassment becomes harder to identify (and prosecute) when the infractions are less obvious. If a female supervisor continues to ask an employee out on a date after he has already told her he is not interested, or a woman feels that a male colleague stares at her inappropriately, there is less agreement on whether a legal line has been crossed. Jokes that may be offensive to one woman but not offensive to her female coworkers are yet another example of the difficulties in drawing clear lines.

A key component to stopping harassing behavior early is communication. For instance, a woman can reduce the likelihood of harassment and establish what she believes to be appropriate behavior by being firm when she is offended. Speaking up and making sure your opinion is heard can go a long way in helping others to understand what you consider appropriate. If someone puts an arm around you as a form of greeting, and the act makes you uncomfortable, then a firm, "I'd prefer that you not put your arm around me," may take care of the problem. You have established a boundary. If the behavior reoccurs, then perhaps you should involve a teacher or the principal.

SEXUAL ABUSE IN COMMUNITY INSTITUTIONS

A 2002 article in the *Child Abuse Review* points out the growing number of scandals involving professionals who used their work to target and sexually abuse children in the course of the previous 15 years. Similar discoveries have been made in care for the aged. If, as A. Nicholas Groth and other psychologists have stated, sexual abuse is more about power than sex, it is not surprising that those who are least able to defend themselves are targeted.

Establishing firm statistics on the size of the problem of abuse in general and sexual abuse in particular is difficult. Shame and fear may keep many young victims from coming forward. These same feelings may keep elderly people silent as well. In addition, many people suffer from dementia—the loss of mental capacity—as they age. They may not be believed when they report abuse. Statistics cover only the number of abuse cases reported or the number of cases verified and these represent only the tip of the iceberg.

A 1997 report by the Illinois Department of Aging's Elder Abuse and Neglect program defined elder sexual abuse as coercing an older person, through force, trickery, threats, or some other means, into sexual contact against his or her will. In 1995, the program's telephone hotline received 209 reports of sex abuse out of a total of 5,000 calls—roughly 4 percent. The report points out that those calls also had the highest rate of "not verified" results among the various types of mistreatment reported.

A 2004 report to the British Parliament showed that 3 percent of calls to a national abuse hotline reported sexual mistreatment. It was the only growing category in the study. Interestingly, a suggested reason for the growth was that sexual predators who had previously focused on children now found themselves under heavier scrutiny and may have shifted their attention to a less-protected population.

The Kansas Elder Law Network (now the National Elder Law Network) collects research on topics related to the elderly. Although the network has not been able to establish a single profile for abusers or their victims in elder abuse cases, it has established some common findings. Abusers tend to be nursing aides or orderlies who are experiencing burnout and have lost their sense of caring for the patients they serve. Facilities that have few staff to handle many patients are more likely to have cases of abuse. Abusers also tend to be young men with low levels of education and a lack of employment experience. In almost all cases, the victim is either mentally or physically unable to fight off an attacker or report the abuse. Only when a family member recognizes the abuse is it reported.

In 2001, the National Child Abuse and Neglect Data System stated that 903,000 cases of child abuse had been verified out of some 5 million reports. Of these verified cases, 9.6 percent involved sexual abuse. A 2000 article in the publication *British Association of Social Workers* discussed the particular vulnerability of children to sexual abuse in institutional settings such as foster homes, clubs, schools, churches and synagogues, playgrounds, and family centers. In too many of these settings, sexual predators can establish themselves as caregivers or authority figures—coaches, teachers, religious leaders, or activity directors. By giving extra attention to children or promising candy, money, alcohol, or other enticements, they may lead children into an abusive situation.

Sexual violence is a difficult subject to understand in terms of the extent of the problem, the issues victims face, and even the importance of the crime. For example, the U.S. Supreme Court ruled against a law that established the death penalty for rapists on the grounds that victims survived the abuse. The question that remained unanswered was how the crime had impacted the lives of those survivors.

See also: Family Violence; Suicide

FURTHER READING
Lindquist, S. *The Date Rape Prevention Book: The Essential Guide for Girls and Women.* Napierville, Ill.: Sourcebooks, Inc., 2000.

■ SOCIAL COSTS OF VIOLENCE

The price a society pays for crime and other violent behaviors. Some of that cost is financial, such as the loss people must deal with when thieves steal the family car or robbers make off with thousands of dollars from a bank or an armored truck. Taxpayers also pay; they finance efforts to prevent and punish crimes. Human costs are also associated with violence, including physical pain, mental suffering, and in some cases, loss of life.

The most recent comprehensive financial figures related to the price American society pays for violence comes from *The Cost of Violent Crime*, a 1994 report by the Bureau of Justice Statistics. In 1992, the nation lost more than $17 billion. Some of those losses were due to robberies, but far more money was associated with medical expenses, property damage, lost pay due to missing work, and production losses.

Costs resulting from the commission of a crime can vary considerably depending on the source. Taking an average of the amounts lost in the 324,938 robberies reported in 2002, the Bureau of Justice Statistics report *Crime Victimization 2003* placed a value of $1,281 per robbery. Compare that to the $19,200 cost associated with a robbery in the 1993 book *Understanding and Preventing Violence*. According to this work, only 15 percent of the costs were financial—the monetary loss, society's loss of a worker's production, and emergency response to the crime. The rest represent nonmonetary losses including pain, suffering, risk of death, and psychological damage.

In its Web site on crime victims and civil justice, the National Center for Victims of crime estimates that in 2004, crimes cost victims $345 billion.

ENFORCEMENT COSTS

Many of the costs of protecting a community are connected to its rate of violence. Essentially, as the rate of violence rises, so does the cost of police work. The U.S. Department of Justice 2001 annual report counted 441,000 officers in local police departments. Monetary support for those officers was $36.7 billion, or an average of about $80,000 per person. That money includes not only salary, but also the cost of training, operating facilities, non-officer support staff, automobiles, equipment, and general operation expenses. Based on the number of people in the United States, Americans spend approximately $179 per resident on local police. In addition, the report tabulated 200,000 law enforcement officers on the state level, and 93,000 federal agents authorized to make arrests.

The *Sourcebook of Criminal Justice Statistics 2002* issued by the Department of Justice looked at the figures differently. This report estimated the total expenditures for the justice system on the federal, state, and local level at more than $146.5 billion. Police protection accounted for less than half that figure (a little over $65 billion).

MEDICAL COSTS

The Cost of Violent Crime noted that 31 percent of the 1.4 million victims of violent crime (assault, robbery, and rape) required medical care. How much did that care cost? Consider the cost of gunshot wounds alone. A 1999 article in the *Journal of the American Medical Association* estimated that each gunshot injury in the United States costs an average of $17,000. Those wounds were also responsible for $2.3 billion in medical costs over the patients' lifetime. Of that amount, 49 percent, or $1.1 billion, came from taxpayers.

Violence that occurs between intimate partners cost almost $6 billion in 2003, according to the Centers for Disease Control and Prevention (CDC). Most of that cost, a little over $45 billion, went to direct medical care for victims of domestic violence. The remaining $2 billion was attributed to lost pay, lost production, and costs connected to the deaths of those who did not survive the violence.

PROSECUTION, INCARCERATION, AND REHABILITATION COSTS

In a 2002 report by the Department of Justice, officials stated that expenditures for the criminal justice system exceeded $146 billion. Included in that number was spending by governments at various levels to provide police protection, operate and monitor correctional facilities, and fund judicial and legal activities.

The federal government spent about $8 billion on the criminal justice system, while state governments spent more than $12.8 billion, and local governments over $14 billion.

The costs of incarceration, or confinement in a jail or prison, are not as simple to determine as it might seem. On the federal level, corrections expenditures came to more than $4 billion. State prisons cost $34.7 million to run, while local governments spent $15 billion on jails.

According to the Office of National Drug Control Policy, the cost of incarcerating an inmate at a federal prison is $23,542 per year, while incarceration at the state level averages $20,261 per year. These costs include the expense of building prisons and operating them.

However, there are other costs that most people don't think about. Every benefit that a prisoner could potentially add to his or her community but cannot because of incarceration is considered a social cost. It includes the wages a prisoner might have earned if he or she was in society working and the value of what that prisoner might have produced on the job. The social costs also include the effects of incarceration on the prisoner's family, particularly on his or her children.

Fact Or Fiction?

Society doesn't owe criminals anything while they're in prison. They can sit and rot.

Fact: While rotting in prison might punish an offender, that approach will hardly prepare an inmate for life after prison—or help to keep a former inmate from criminal activity that will guarantee a trip *back* to prison.

Providing rehabilitation services for people in prison serves both the inmate and the larger community. Helping prisoners develop skills to become productive members of society or learning a trade improve the prospects both for the inmate and the community.

In a 1982 survey researchers from the Rand Corporation interviewed prisoners on their criminal behavior. They found that on average, the inmates committed 200 crimes a year. However, because a small number of prisoners committed an extremely high number of crimes, they threw the average off. When researchers looked for the midpoint in the number of crimes committed, it came out to 17.

A 2001 study of rehabilitation programs in the *Journal of Research on Crime and Delinquency* found that these efforts reduced the rate at which former prisoners returned to prison by 20 percent. Considering the vast prison population in the United States, imagine how many crimes rehabilitation may prevent.

Many prisons in communities across the United States have designed programs to help inmates overcome addictions or develop the skills necessary to remain free from crime. Some are self-help programs that assist prisoners in dealing with addiction or behavior problems. **Guided self-help programs** allow people to work on problems by themselves with information or advice from a therapist, a book, or a computer program.

Some prisons provide **group therapy,** a form of psychological treatment in which participants, with the help of a therapist, meet regularly to analyze their own and one another's problems. The interaction among the participants is an important part of the treatment process. **Individual self-help** allows inmates to deal with problems in their lives by learning to receive help, give help, and help themselves. Groups such as Alcoholics Anonymous have worked on the principle of individual self-help for years.

Many prisoners develop skills in communication, learning how to manage anger and avoid conflict. Some inmates even go out into the community to talk with young people about their experiences in prison. Kansas has a program that has seen the recidivism rate of inmates (the rate of people returning to prison after discharge) in such programs drop to one-half the national rate.

Q & A

Question: What factor has the largest effect on increasing the prison population?

Answer: Alcohol and substance abuse play the largest part in landing people in prison. According to the Office of National Drug Control Policy, $30 billion of the $38 billion dollars spent on housing inmates in 1996 was spent on people with a history of drug use who were either convicted of drug violations, who were drunk or high at the time of their crime, or who committed the crime to get money for drugs.

Because alcohol and other forms of drug abuse are associated with many violent crimes, a number of prisons run programs for **drug rehabilitation,** a general term for programs and activities that help drug users overcome their addiction. According to the Office of National Drug Control Policy (ONDCP), 21 percent of all inmates in 1998 were drug offenders. An article appearing in the 2002 book *Treatment of Drug Offenders* pointed out that in-prison treatment centers are inexpensive compared to outpatient, community-based treatment. Reviewing three prison-based programs, researchers found that the cost per inmate ranged from $37 to $68 per week, while community treat-

DID YOU KNOW?

Estimated Social Costs of Selected Crimes

Crime	Estimated Social Cost, 1999
Rape	$98,327
Assault	$10,624
Robbery	$8,830
Motor vehicle theft	$3,249
Burglary	$1,271
Fraud, forgery, petty theft	$342
Drug sale	$5

(Adjusted data from the National Institute of Justice)

Source: Manhattan Institute for Policy Research, 1999.

ment programs averaged over $600 per week. The ONDCP also empha-sizes the importance of treatment, reporting that for every dollar spent on treating an inmate for addiction, the community benefits by three dollars, tripling the value of the treatment. These programs benefit communities by reducing the costs associated with crime and also by turning prison inmates into productive citizens.

The social costs of violence can be counted in billions of dollars and measured in the months of often painful medical treatment for survivors of violent crimes. Less easily measured is the fear that pre-vents people from attending an event that take place after dark or requires a trip through a dangerous neighborhood. The most painful statistic is the tens of thousands of people who pay the ultimate cost—losing their lives to violent crime.

TEENS SPEAK

Counting the Costs

Duane is 17, having spent the last four years as an inmate after being convicted of aggravated assault.

"I was 13 when a kid from school dissed me bad, and I beat him till he couldn't stand up. That got me four years."

He looks around the bare, institutional room. "So what did it cost? Time. Time with my family, as messed up as it is, it's still all I have. Time with my friends, my girl. They all forgot me. There isn't really a school here. The best I'll get is a General Education Degree (GED). My former friends are getting ready for college, and I'm here, falling farther behind.

"They have cars, I sit here. They have money, I sit here. They go wherever they want, and I freaking sit here." He smashes a fist into the thin mattress on his cot.

"You know what's weird? I'm scared to leave now. In here, I know the routine, I'm used to it. Out there, I have no life, and it scares me to have to start over.

"My advice? Listen to people. Sounds crazy, I know, but it would have made a difference. Listen when they tell you that what you think is cool really isn't. Listen when they warn you about people who will screw up your life. Listen when they tell you they love you, because you won't want to, and then they're gone. That's not cool."

See also: Alcohol and Violence; Criminals and Violent Activity; Drugs and Violence; Weapons of Violence

FURTHER READING
Harris Terrell, Ruth. *A Kid's Guide on How to Stop the Violence.* New York: Avon, 1992.

■ SUICIDE

The intentional taking of one's own life. In 2002, the *Sourcebook of Criminal Justice Statistics* reported 12.4 suicides per 100,000 people in the United States. The rate was higher for those 80 years and older, with over 19 deaths per 100,000. According to the Health Central Web site, while Americans over the age of 60 make up only 13 percent of the population, they accounted for 18 percent of all suicides in 2000.

Statistics from the Centers for Disease Control and Prevention (CDC) named suicide as the 11th-highest cause of death in 2000.

Although the suicide rate has declined slightly among teens since 1992, it was the third-leading cause of death among young people ages 15 to 24 in 2001.

Completed suicides are only part of the problem. More people are hospitalized or treated and released as a result of suicide attempts than are fatally injured. While suicide is often viewed as a response to a single stressful event, it is a far more complicated issue.

CAUSES OF SUICIDE

Suicides are not caused by a single factor but by a combination of factors. **Depression** plays an important role in many suicides. About 75 percent of those who commit suicide are depressed. People often mistake depression for "feeling blue." Depression is more than a little sadness. It is caused by a number of factors ranging from chemical imbalances to environmental influences. A person with depression is likely to display one or more of the following behaviors:

- Feelings of worthlessness, hopelessness, helplessness, total indifference, or unreasonable guilt
- Prolonged sadness; unexplained crying spells
- Jumpiness or irritability
- Withdrawal from formerly enjoyable activities or relationships
- Inability to concentrate or remember details; indecisiveness
- Noticeable change in appetite with sudden weight loss or gain
- Changes in sleep patterns: constant fatigue, insomnia, early waking, oversleeping
- Physical ailments that cannot be otherwise explained

According to the Harris County Psychiatric Center at the University of Texas, other contributing factors to suicides and attempted suicides may include:

- Substance abuse
- Divorce of parents
- Parental unemployment
- Financial problems

- Isolation from family or friends
- Rejection by a boyfriend or girlfriend
- Domestic violence or abuse
- Lack of success at school

Q & A

Question: Aren't most suicides committed by women?

Answer: In 1999, the surgeon general, the highest-ranking public health officer in the country, reported that females are more likely to attempt suicide, but men are more likely to die from their attempts. In 1996, white males accounted for 73 percent of all suicides in the United States.

Among the statistics collected by the University of California, Los Angeles (UCLA) was that more than half of all suicide victims were males between the ages of 25 to 65.

PREVALENCE AMONG YOUNG PEOPLE

According to statistics published by the Centers for Disease Control and Prevention (CDC) on the major causes of death among young people, only unintentional injuries—mostly car crashes—and murder are responsible for more deaths among teens. Every two years since 1991, the CDC has conducted a nationwide survey of students in grades nine through 12 to assess attitudes that might affect their health. The Youth Risk Behavior Surveillance System (YRBSS) is a nationwide survey conducted every other year of students in grades nine through 12. In the 2003 YRBSS, 28.6 percent of the teens surveyed reported feeling sad or hopeless almost every day for two weeks. In the 12 months before the survey, 16.9 percent considered suicide. In that same time period, 16.5 percent of the students actually planned a suicide. Approximately half that number—8.5 percent—went as far as attempting to kill themselves.

Teens can be especially susceptible to suicidal thoughts. Adolescents experience dramatic biochemical changes. Sudden mood swings are common. As their sexuality emerges, teens are faced with new experiences, feelings, and challenges. These sometimes disorienting changes can be complicated by substance abuse.

The teen years are also often filled with intensive self-examination. Young people often ask themselves, "Who am I?" or "Why don't I fit in?" These questions can lead some people into despair, especially if they are already experiencing depression or other mental disorders.

Another element that makes being a teenager especially difficult is the realization that one is about to become an adult. As a child, one feels like an extension of his or her parents. As an adolescent, once-respected adults are now authority figures who seem to want the teenager to stay a child forever. Many wish their parents would do more than just tell them what they can't do. These changes in the relationship between teens and their parents can lead to heated discussions and disagreements. Hurt feelings on both sides are common and can cause emotional distress.

Some young people are idealistic. They have high moral and ethical standards that they would like everyone to live up to. Life is not perfect. Bad things happen. No one is perfect. People make mistakes. Those who are particularly idealistic may be disturbed or disappointed by life's ups and downs.

Community loss—the tragedy of September 11, the loss of the Columbia shuttle, the war in Afghanistan and Iraq—can have devastating effects. If a person is already feeling things are hopeless, it's easy to see tragedies as evidence that nothing and no one is safe.

SUICIDE INTERVENTION

The best time to intervene in suicidal behavior is before a person actually makes a physical attempt. An article published by the Centers for Disease Control and Prevention describes a number of programs that aim at suicide prevention.

Many programs use the concept of a **gatekeeper,** a person trained to recognize individuals who are at risk and offer help. At school, a gatekeeper could be a teacher, counselor, or coach. Some programs also teach these and other staff members how to deal with suicides and other crises at their schools. Gatekeepers can also be recruited from the community, including clergy, police, staff members at recreation facilities, and doctors and nurses who provide health care for young people.

Some programs are aimed directly at students. These programs alert them to the warning signs of a potential suicide and how to get help for themselves or others. Other programs are designed to help students feel better about themselves and improve their social skills.

Identifying young people at risk for suicide may require screening programs. Such efforts use questionnaires or other means to identify possible suicidal attitudes. Screening can also be used to track changes in outlook and behavior, or even to evaluate the effectiveness of other suicide prevention projects.

Peer support programs can be organized both inside and outside schools, allowing students or young people to work together, helping one another and learning to help themselves. Such programs may help to break the isolation often experienced by young people at risk. These programs may also help them learn better social skills.

The program most often featured in the media is the telephone hotline or crisis center. Here, trained volunteers and paid professional staff offer counseling over the phone or face-to-face. Such programs often include referrals to mental health services.

Access restriction programs seek to keep those who wish to take their own life from potential weapons such as guns, drugs, or poisons. Other programs offer a plan of action after a suicide has occurred. These responses are usually aimed at friends and relatives of those who have committed suicide. In part, the effort is to avoid suicide clusters—attempts to copy the initial suicide. In addition, these programs may help young people cope with their feelings of loss at the death of a friend or peer.

Fact Or Fiction?

Suicide victims are all wound up in their private little worlds.

Fact: Suicide may be an intensely personal decision, but that decision is affected by events in the larger world. Suicide clusters occur when two or more individuals try to copy the suicide of someone they know or have heard about through media coverage. A 2001 article in the *British Journal of Psychology* discussed the reaction to the 1997 death of Princess Diana, a well-known public figure. Researchers examined suicide figures for the month following her funeral and compared them with suicide rates for the same period of time over the prior five years. They found 17.4 percent more suicides after the funeral, especially among women, with a total increase of 33.7 percent. Young women, ages 24 to 44 were especially affected, with a higher suicide rate of 45.1 percent.

RECOGNIZING THE SIGNS

Suicides do not happen without warning. Most people give clues or talk about their feelings before acting upon them. Recognizing and responding to these clues can prevent suicide attempts and death. Teens who are considering suicide are likely to:

- Talk about or seem preoccupied with death; say things like "My family would be better off without me" or "I wish I were dead"
- Lose interest in important or pleasurable activities
- Do poorly in school
- Show signs and symptoms of depression
- Give away important possessions, clean their rooms, and throw things away
- Neglect hygiene and self-care
- Withdraw from relationships, family or friends
- Behave recklessly, take high risks
- Abuse drugs and/or alcohol

Everyone experiences difficulties in life and may show one or more of these behaviors. However, when these behaviors form a pattern, they should not be ignored. Often, having the opportunity to speak to a sympathetic listener can help prevent a suicide. Essentially, that is the principle behind suicide telephone hotlines.

If a friend or acquaintance speaks seriously about suicide, do not keep silent. Remain calm and recognize your friend's conversation for what it is—a plea for help. Do not attempt to solve the problem on your own. Express your concerns for your friend's safety or state of mind to a teacher or counselor.

For many, suicide is a particularly distressing form of violence. The waste of a life—especially a young life—by one's own hand has a tragic effect on those the suicide victim leaves behind. Educating oneself about suicide, participating in suicide intervention programs, and staying open to friends and peers can make a difference.

See also: Alcohol and Violence; Assault and Bullying; Media and Violence; School Violence; Teens and Violence

FURTHER READING
Wallerstein, Claire. *Teen Suicide.* Chicago: Heinemann Library, 2003.

■ TEENS AND VIOLENCE

The connection between teens and violence—crime, gang violence, or fights—has worried Americans for many years, as shown by extensive media coverage on the subject. A sharp increase approximately 20 years ago resulted in greater public awareness and concern. A 2001 special report by the surgeon general, the nation's highest-ranking public health officer, stated, "The epidemic of youth violence that began in 1983 and peaked in 1993 is not over. Arrest rates for violent crimes by youth have dropped significantly since 1993, giving cause for hope, but other indicators of violent behavior remain high."

The report cited three major reasons for the surge in violence: a growth in gang membership, involvement of young people in the sale of illegal drugs, and the use of guns.

The Centers for Disease Control and Prevention (CDC) described the impact of those factors in its 2001–2002 Injury Fact Book. It noted that teens and young adults tend to act impulsively and engage in risk-taking behaviors. Add a deadly weapon like a gun to impulsive behavior and the results can be extremely risky—even fatal.

VICTIMS OF VIOLENCE

According to the CDC, more than 877,700 young people ages 10 to 24 were injured from violent acts in 2002. Approximately one in 13 required hospitalization. One of the tools the government uses to assess dangers to young people is a national survey made every other year of students in grades nine to 12. Results of the 2003 Youth Risk Behavior Surveillance System (YRBSS) showed that 17.1 percent of the students surveyed had carried a weapon in the previous month, including 6.1 percent who had carried a gun. In the year prior to the survey, 33 percent of the students had gotten into a fight, and 4.2 of them were injured sufficiently enough that they needed medical treatment.

For several years, the CDC has identified homicide as the second-leading cause of death for people aged 15 to 24, and the leading cause of death for African Americans in the same age group. The Bureau of Justice Statistics reports that 16- to 19-year-olds are more likely than other Americans to experience a violent crime.

Examination of statistics for violent crimes in the National Crime Victimization Survey shows a similar pattern. People under the age of 24 are more likely to be victims of murder, rape, robbery, and aggravated assault than those who are over 24.

In 2003, one in three murder victims in the United States was under 25. One in five of all rape victims were between 18 and 21. One-half of all robberies happened to people under the age of 21. One-half of all aggravated assault victims was younger than 25. Young people in this nation make up the majority of the victims of violent activity.

Dating violence victims

Dating violence refers to physical or sexual abuse by a date or acquaintance. It also includes verbal threats, intimidation, and emotional abuse. A 2001 article in the *Journal of the American Medical Association* stated that approximately 20 percent of adolescent girls have reported being physically or sexually hurt by a dating partner.

In 1995, the advocacy organization Children Now and the Kaiser Permanente insurance group commissioned a national poll on youth safety. Among girls age 14 to 17, 40 percent reported knowing someone their age who had been hit or beaten by a boyfriend. A 1997 survey on the health of adolescent girls by the Commonwealth Fund found that 26 percent of girls in grades nine to 12 had been victims of physical abuse, sexual abuse, or date rape.

Victims of bullying

The Center for the Study and Prevention of Violence at the University of Colorado at Boulder has identified two primary types of victims of bullying. First is the passive or submissive victim, and the second is called the provocative victim. Passive victims send out the message that they are weak or insecure and that they will probably not fight back if they are bullied. The provocative victim can be either anxious or aggressive in dealing with their classmates.

Fact Or Fiction?

Bullying is just a part of growing up.

Fact: A study by the advocacy group Kids First found that children who had been bullied grow up to be sadder than others, with lower self-esteem. They have been known to turn violence inward by committing suicide and outward by harming others. Three-quarters of the young shooters in recent cases of school gun violence were victims of bullying.

Bullies face difficulties as adults as well. Scandinavian researchers, who were among the first to pay scientific attention to bullying, conducted a long-term study. By their mid-20s, young men who had been identified by classmates as bullies had significantly more trouble with the law. Among the former bullies, 60 percent had been convicted of a crime, compared to a crime rate of 23 percent among those who had not shown bullying behavior. In addition, 35 to 40 percent of the former bullies had three convictions, compared to only 10 percent of those in the non-bullying group.

The center lists the following characteristics for passive/submissive victims:

- Are physically weaker than their peers (particularly boys)
- Display "body anxiety." They are afraid of being hurt, have poor physical coordination, and are ineffective in physical play or sports
- Have poor social skills and have difficulty making friends
- Are cautious, sensitive, quiet, withdrawn, and shy
- Cry or become upset easily
- Are anxious, insecure, and have poor self-esteem
- Have difficulty standing up for or defending themselves in peer groups
- Relate better to adults than to peers

Provocative victims display these characteristics:

- Exhibit some or all of the characteristics of passive or submissive victims
- Are hot-tempered and attempt to fight back when victimized—usually not effectively
- Are hyperactive, restless, have difficulty concentrating, and create tension
- Are clumsy, immature, and exhibit irritating habits
- Are also disliked by adults, including teachers
- Try to bully students weaker than themselves

The experience of being bullied can have severe consequences. Victims may develop feelings of low self-worth and even turn to suicide.

Victims of hate crimes

Hate crimes are crimes prompted by an individual's race, religion, sexual orientation, gender, ethnic or national origin, or disability. These crimes aim to terrorize an entire community. In 2001, the Federal Bureau of Investigation's Uniform Crime Reporting program reported on 9,730 hate crimes. Approximately 65 percent of these were directed against an individual, including simple assault (without a weapon), aggravated assault, rape, and murder. Crimes against property (robbery, vandalism, destroying, stealing, or setting fire to vehicles, homes, stores, and places of worship) accounted for approximately 35 percent of these crimes. Additional forms of abuse included threats by mail, telephone, or e-mail.

Q & A

Question: Why do so many teens get involved with drugs and guns?

Answer: As the American Prosecutors Resource Institute points out, the involvement of young people in the drug trade resulted from a cold-blooded business decision by drug dealers. During the 1980s, many states adopted new laws with stern punishments for drug sales. Dealers began to recruit young people, who face less serious penalties in juvenile court. With the explosion in sales of crack, a cheap form of cocaine, many of these young "apprentices" started dealing themselves—and carrying guns to protect their merchandise and money.

PERPETRATORS OF VIOLENCE

According to the surgeon general's *Special Report on Youth Violence*, arrest rates for violent crimes have declined since 1994, primarily due to fewer young people using guns. A number of factors were cited as contributing to this reduction—a decline in youth involvement in the crack cocaine market, police crackdowns on gun carrying, a strong

DID YOU KNOW?

Percentage of High School Students Who Carried a Gun or Other Weapon, by Ethnicity, Sex, and Grade

	Carried a Weapon			Carried a Gun		
	Female	Male	Total	Female	Male	Total
Race/Ethnicity						
White	5.5	27.1	16.7	1.5	10.0	5.9
Black	9.8	24.9	17.3	1.4	10.6	6.0
Hispanic	8.5	24.3	16.5	2.6	8.2	5.4
Grade						
9	8.8	26.6	18.0	2.1	9.3	5.8
10	5.2	26.5	15.9	1.4	10.4	5.9
11	6.8	29.2	18.2	1.6	10.8	6.3
12	5.2	25.2	15.5	1.0	10.0	5.7
Total	6.7	26.9	17.1	1.6	10.2	6.1

Source: Youth Risk Behavior Surveillance System, 2003.

economy, and crime and violence prevention programs. However, many other indicators of youth violence remain high. Arrest rates for aggravated assaults are nearly 70 percent higher than they were in 1983, and self-reporting studies indicate that the proportion of young people involved in violent behavior and the rates of violent offending have not declined since the mid-1990s.

The National Center for Injury Prevention and Control has identified factors that put young people at risk for becoming violent. In general, adolescent males are much more likely to be violent than females. An early history of acting aggressively can predict later violence, especially if youthful violence involves **antisocial behavior**—a repeated pattern of disregard for and violation of the rights of others. Antisocial behavior often includes fighting, habitual lying, reckless disregard for the safety of others, and acts like setting fires or hurting animals. Another sign of later aggressiveness is the individual's belief that violence is acceptable behavior.

Perpetrators of sexual violence in dating tend to believe that men are supposed to be independent and competitive and women dependent and supportive. Based on these beliefs, some young males may attempt to "prove their manhood" through violence and sexual conquests. They are likely to choose friends who are also sexually aggressive and accept the use of violence to resolve some relationship conflicts.

TEENS SPEAK

Just Business

Raul is 14 years old. He is presently in custody awaiting trial on drug possession charges.

"It started when I was 10 years old. This guy called Hitter used to come and watch us playing hoops. He'd pass me 50 bucks to hang and play ball. Everybody knew he was dealing—as his stuff looked fine.

"Soon I was helping him out—watching on the street for cops. Three hundred dollars a week, just for looking out for cops in their big old unmarked Chevies." He grins and shakes his head.

"After a while, I began selling on the street for Hitter. It was cool. Nobody paid much attention to me out there 'cause I'm kinda short and looked young. They all called me 'Baby Face.'

"I was doing really well—six hundred a week in my pocket. Hitter started me moving some serious weight. I'd be carrying thirty grand worth of merchandise. That's when I got a gun."

Raul's round face goes tight and grim. "But now that the cops caught me with dope and a gun, they're talking about charging me as an adult. Even if I get lucky and they treat me like a kid, they're gonna ship me off someplace far away from the hood."

Suddenly, he looks very young. "And this is all I know."

Using alcohol and other drugs is highly related to violence, especially suicide. A study reported by the National Clearinghouse on Alcohol and Drug Information on shared characteristics of suicide victims found that 70 percent of these people abused alcohol or drugs. Having a history of bullying or being bullied is related to being violent. Many bullying victims consider suicide.

Youths who are poorly supervised at home or are exposed to violence are more likely to become violent themselves. Students who have lost interest in school or have experienced failure in school are also more likely to show violent behavior. Finally, adolescents who have access to firearms are more likely to use them to perpetrate violence.

The surgeon general's report on youth violence revealed several factors that can predict whether an adolescent will become violent. For teens between the ages of 12 and 14, weak connections to family and the community were strong predictors of violent behavior. Other strong predictors included having friends who had trouble in school or with the law and gang membership.

The National School Safety Center has offered a checklist of characteristics of students most likely to become violent at school. Their list is a result of tracking school-based violent incidents for more than 20 years. Characteristics include:

- History of tantrums and uncontrollable angry outbursts
- Resorting to name-calling, cursing, or abusive language
- Habitually making violent threats when angry
- Having previously brought a weapon to school
- Background of discipline problems at school
- Background of substance abuse or dependency
- Few or no close friends in peer group
- Preoccupation with weapons or explosives
- Displaying cruelty to animals
- Little or no adult supervision outside of school
- Witnessing or being a victim of neglect or abuse
- Having been bullied or bullying others
- Blaming others for problems in his/her life
- Preferring TV, movies, and games that have violent themes

- Preferring reading materials with violent themes
- Reflecting anger, frustration, and the dark side of life in school essays or writings
- Involvement in a gang or social group outside the peer norm
- Often feeling depressed or showing mood swings
- Threatening or attempting suicide

The teenage years are only a fraction of an American's potential lifespan of 70 years or more. Unfortunately, for too many young people this brief experience is colored by conflict. All they know is violence. The problem with following a violent lifestyle, however, is that it may be all too short, ending painfully and abruptly.

See also: Alcohol and Violence; Assault and Bullying; Media and Violence; School Violence

FURTHER READING
Barbour, Scott. *Teen Violence.* San Diego, Calif.: Greenhaven Press, 1999.

■ TERRORISM
See: War

■ VICTIMIZATION
See: Social Costs of Violence

■ VIOLENCE, RANDOM
See: Communities and Violence

■ VIOLENCE PREVENTION
See: Communities and Violence

■ VIOLENT BEHAVIOR, CAUSES OF

Factors that may influence a person to act aggressively. The causes of violence seem to relate to genetics, family influence, social skill development, psychological impairments, hormones, steroids, and social influences.

HEREDITARY INFLUENCES

To answer the question of whether violent behavior is inherited, scientists must establish the existence of a specific **gene** that makes some people violent and others nonviolent. Present estimates suggest that a human has between 28,000 and 120,000 genes. No one has found real evidence to date that a single gene or combination of genes predicts violent behavior.

Evidence does exist suggesting that one's genetic makeup does predict some aspects of one's personality. Humans may inherit personality traits that make them more prone to violent behavior under certain conditions. The idea, however, that a single gene causes someone to be violent is not supported by research.

Fact Or Fiction?

Youth violence isn't a problem. The crime rate is going down.

Fact: Rates for violent crime, specifically homicide, have dropped. That decline is mainly in gun-related violence, which rose sharply in the mid-1990s. Analysis of FBI crime reports shows that once gun-related cases are removed, rates of violent crime are relatively unchanged over a 20-year period.

LEARNED OR ENVIRONMENTAL INFLUENCES

Because no direct link between genes and violence has been discovered, researchers think environment plays an important role in determining whether people become violent. In a sense, violence is a learned behavior.

In 1999, Laurence Steinberg, a social scientist who studies violent behavior, addressed the Working Group on Youth Violence established by the U.S. House of Representatives. Steinberg identified family relationships as the major factor in predicting mental health problems among children and adolescents. Parents who show hostility toward their children or who neglect them create young people at risk for mental problems. These problems may lead to antisocial behaviors, a disregard for the rights of others, persistent violations of rules, and ultimately to violence.

When young children experience or witness violence in their homes or neighborhoods, they learn to associate all conflict of any sort with violence. For them, violence becomes the first response to disagreement or frustration. They come to regard aggressiveness as accepted, even normal behavior. As they grow older, acting on aggressive impulses may lead to violent and even criminal behavior.

Steinberg was involved in a 10-year study of 20,000 adolescents. According to a 2000 issue of the *National Institute of Justice Journal*, he and other researchers found that students who experienced the most problems with school, friends, violence, or the law had parents who were not involved in their children's lives.

A 1997 article in the *Journal of Children and Society* reported similar findings, based on interviews with young offenders. The young offenders described seeing their parents display poor judgment and violent behavior in relationships. They also admitted feeling unloved, neglected, and not understood by their parents. As Dr. Steinberg explained in his congressional testimony, for parents to successfully rear children who become healthy adults, the children must be the priority.

PSYCHOLOGICAL IMPAIRMENTS

Certain patterns of behavior suggest that aggressive individuals face some psychological challenges. In a 1997 study in the journal *Suicide and Life Threatening Behavior*, researchers determined that adolescents hospitalized for aggression or attempted suicide were more likely to have unrealistic views of their health. Their anxiety and levels of fear were abnormally high. Many suffered from paranoia, a psychological disorder characterized by feelings of persecution, and early stages of schizophrenia, a psychological disorder characterized by a distorted sense of reality. They also suffered from social introversion, a tendency to shrink from social contacts. These diagnoses have become important in predicting whether a person will turn violence inward by harming themselves or turn it outward by striking out against others.

A 1998 article in the *American Journal of Psychiatry* reported a study of 313 people diagnosed with severe mental illnesses.

Researchers found that patients' decisions to not take their medications and problems with alcohol or substance abuse were connected to acts of violence.

Researchers also found that yet another factor in weighing the likelihood of violence was whether the patients in the study remained in contact with their health professionals. A 1997 study in the journal *Psychiatry* found that when patients do not maintain regular contact with a mental health provider, feelings of being threatened and out of control increased, as did the likelihood of violent behavior.

A 1992 article in *Phi Delta Kappan* magazine identified a series of nonclinical psychological factors that may influence how aggressive an individual becomes. These included lower levels of intelligence, shyness, acting out as a response to frustration, and an inability to set goals.

Psychological problems can impact other factors to result in an act of violence whether or not a clinical diagnosis exists. The environment again plays a major role in the act of violence. For instance, many people have difficulty setting goals. Not all of them become violent. In fact, only a small percentage does. Those who act out their frustrations do so when they find themselves in unfamiliar or uncomfortable situations. At that point, their inability to set a goal is magnified by their frustration at not meeting some level of expectation, real or imagined. People who have developed social skills and skills in anger management can work through conflict, while for those whose skills are less developed, conflict may become violent.

DEFICIENT SOCIAL SKILLS

An individual's inability to manage conflict often serves as the trigger for an act of violence. No one can avoid conflict entirely. Everyone needs the skills necessary to negotiate tension without violence. Those skills are learned. They include the ability to become closely associated with others, to communicate, control one's anger, cooperate, ask for help when needed, and delay personal gratification.

A 1996 article in *Elementary School Guidance and Counseling* identified the importance of the following skills in addressing aggressive responses in youths:

- Problem solving: the ability to identify the conflict at hand, see a variety of solutions, and choose the one best suited for the situation

- Anger control: the ability to control internal (thought-oriented) anger and external (actions toward others) anger when the time arises through positive self-talk and such physical actions as deep breathing, counting, or walking away.

- Assertiveness: standing up for oneself in situations where one's rights may be violated, but doing so in such a way that one doesn't violate the rights of others

HORMONAL AND BIOLOGICAL INFLUENCES

The idea that there may be a chemical link to violent behavior has received growing support in the scientific community. The human body contains many chemicals, including **hormones,** substances that initiate and stop body processes and even emotions. A hormonal imbalance can affect a person's mood and emotions.

In her 1996 article on the causes of violence printed in *Elementary School Guidance and Counseling,* Jeannine Studer points out that the hormones **serotonin** and testosterone may affect violent behaviors. Serotonin is a chemical the brain uses to regulate mood. Low levels of serotonin are most often associated with depression. The relationship between violence and serotonin has been researched in both humans and nonhuman subjects. The possibility of violent behaviors seems to be elevated in individuals who have low levels of serotonin. The low levels impact their ability to manage emotions (like depression and anger).

Testosterone is a hormone connected with sex differences. The reason men tend to be more aggressive than women is often attributed to the higher levels of testosterone in men. Studer notes, however, that low levels of serotonin and high levels of testosterone in and of themselves do not predict violence. Environmental factors usually trigger violent acts, and abnormal levels of these two hormones may make some people more likely to physically express their anger.

Steroids are hormonelike substances chemically similar to testosterone. Androgenic steroids are actually based on testosterone, while anabolic steroids are synthetic forms of the hormone. Testosterone, of course, has been linked with the higher levels of aggressiveness in males. By dosing themselves with steroids in the hope of increasing muscle mass and endurance, men magnify the amount of testosterone

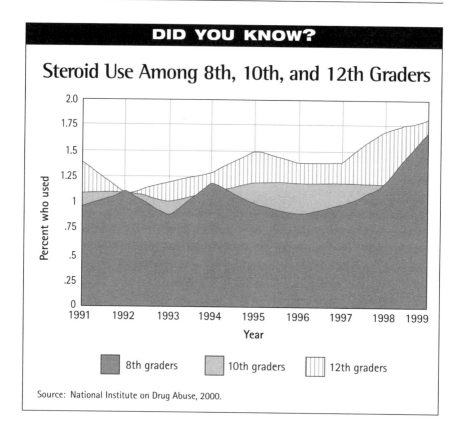

DID YOU KNOW?

Steroid Use Among 8th, 10th, and 12th Graders

Percent who used — Year

8th graders   10th graders   12th graders

Source: National Institute on Drug Abuse, 2000.

in their system. Such magnification increases the degree of aggression in individuals taking the drug.

The Monitoring the Future survey, a yearly poll conducted by the National Institute on Drug Abuse (NIDA), tracked the growth in steroid use in the 1990s. In 2003, the survey reported that 2.5 percent of eighth graders, 3 percent of 10th graders, and 3.5 percent of 12th graders had used steroids at some point in their lives. However, since steroid use is illegal, the real percentage may be much higher.

A survey by the Centers for Disease Control and Prevention (CDC) of high school students in Louisiana found that 12 percent of the boys and 5.7 percent of the girls used steroids. In establishing a campaign against steroid abuse, the head of the NIDA estimated that about 500,000 eighth and 10th graders used these performance-enhancing drugs. The University of Michigan Health System claims that at least 1 million Americans have tried steroids.

Steroids have serious side effects. In men, they can cause liver and kidney damage, development of breasts, acne, baldness, cysts, sterility, and reduced sex drive. In women, steroid use can prevent pregnancy, cause breasts to atrophy, develop menstrual irregularities, and develop male-pattern baldness and the deepening of the voice.

Another side effect of the drug is sudden outbursts of anger, or what is commonly referred to as **steroid rage.** Researchers have yet to figure out who is most likely to be affected by this side effect, or even what levels of steroid use will trigger rage.

A 1996 article published in the *Medical Journal of Australia* identified some of the changes that occur at varying levels of steroid use. In the early stages of use confidence, energy, and self-esteem all seemed to increase. Some athletes notice an ability to train despite pain, and even experience an increase in sex drive, but often report an overriding sense of irritation or edginess. As use continues over time and dosages increase, the Australian researchers noticed that users were less likely to show good judgment and were more likely to be impulsive. They also noted an increase in paranoid thoughts and aggressive behavior.

At high dosage levels, the Australian researchers found, users became very aggressive, hostile, violent, and uncontrolled—a danger to themselves and others. In other words, they displayed the signs of steroid rage. These outbursts of anger resulted in property damage, injuries to the users (including reckless driving or crashing cars), assaults, family and intimate violence, child abuse, suicide, and attempted murder or murder.

Another 1996 study refuted these conclusions. Researchers found no change in mood among the 43 men they followed in a clinically controlled study. Each man received 600 milligrams of testosterone each week for 10 weeks. According to the *New England Journal of Medicine,* the researchers measured changes in each subject's strength and whether he became more hostile or easily angered. While they found no change in mood, the researchers admitted that the amount of performance-enhancing drug given was controlled, and the men were screened in advance. If a steroid user was unstable to begin with or took large, uncontrolled dosages, rage was possible. The 600 milligrams of testosterone given the men in the study was six times the normal levels of testosterone in males. However, athletes who use steroids use 10 to 40 times their normal testosterone level, or 4,000 milligrams a week.

Because every individual's body chemistry is different, responses to performance-enhancing drugs may vary. However, the length of time people use steroids and the dosage they take seem to work together to cause the greatest negative effect and the most likely trigger for violent behavior.

Q & A

Question: Don't video games have a rating system to make sure violent games don't wind up in the hands of kids?

Answer: The National Institute on Media and the Family surveyed 778 students, grades four through 12 about video games in 2003. The average age of the young people was 13.5. Some 87 percent of the boys played M-rated games, which are supposedly restricted to players 17 and older. When asked to name their favorite games, 78 percent of the boys listed M-rated games in their top five, and 40 percent said that their favorite game was rated M.

These statistics suggest that many stores are not enforcing the ratings system. Nor are parents doing so. One out of five of the boys in the survey admitted to buying an M-rated game without parental permission.

SOCIETAL INFLUENCE

Social scientists continue to debate whether watching violence in the movies or on TV or reading about it causes a person to act violently. If there were a direct link between the two, wouldn't everyone who watched a violent action film leave the theater and engage in fights, if not murder? As with so many causes of violence, the answer seems to lie in a combination of individual factors, including an individual's predisposition to violence, whether he or she has a nonmedicated mental illness, and the immediate environment.

Many fear that viewing many acts of violence can have a desensitizing effect on individuals, especially young people. Given the amount of violence on the air, some estimate that by the time teens finish high school, they will have seen over 100,000 acts of violence on network television. If they have access to cable television, as most do today, that number is probably much higher.

Video games have also become a regular means of entertainment for youths. A study reported at the 2003 conference of the International Simulation and Game Association polled fifth graders to name their favorite video games. Of the 41 top titles, 85 percent contained violent content.

Turning violence into a part of everyday life, or even enjoyment, has a negative effect on a society. People feel less surprised and outraged when acts of brutality occur in real life. This desensitization may make people less likely to take a stand when they experience a violation of their own rights or see someone else's rights violated.

See also: Communities and Violence; Drugs and Violence; Media and Violence; School Violence; Teens and Violence

FURTHER READING

Langone, John. *Violence! Our Fastest-Growing Health Problem.* Boston: Little, Brown, 1984.

■ WAR

Large-scale organized violence between nations or ethnic groups. Reasons for armed conflict can include political disputes between nations, conflicts between political ideologies, racial or ethnic competition, and religious differences. The United Nations defines a "major war" as a military conflict that inflicts more than 1,000 battlefield casualties per year. At the end of 2003, 15 major wars and at least 20 lesser conflicts were underway around the world. Many of these smaller struggles are civil wars—wars between opposing groups within the same country.

In almost every country, citizens support a military force. In some cases, that force is small and so is the percentage of the national budget devoted to military affairs. Other countries have huge military establishments costing billions of dollars and consuming a significant percentage of national resources. The costs of war quickly move beyond the money needed to pay soldiers, buy guns to put in their hands, and purchase ammunition for those weapons.

Q & A

Question: My brother signed up with the army to get help going to college. Now he's off in the middle of nowhere with a rifle! What can my family do?

Answer: Unfortunately, your brother is learning the difference between a peacetime and wartime army. In the 1990s, many people joined the military for job training or educational benefits. However, the basic job of any military organization is to fight. Your brother may face some difficult, even dangerous times during his tour of duty. It will be up to you and your family to maintain his morale with plenty of letters, messages, and packages from home.

FINANCIAL COSTS OF WAR

War is expensive. War-making involves much more than just the frontline troops, tanks, artillery pieces, and aircraft.

Military action requires transportation to get supplies and reinforcements to the war zone. Military organizations must also provide facilities for existing troops, maintenance shops to repair trucks and tanks, warehouses for equipment and spare parts, and much, much more. World War I cost the United States alone $22.6 billion. The expenses for all of the countries involved in the conflict cost nearly $200 trillion. The *Christian Science Monitor* has estimated that the 2003 war with Iraq may end up costing the United States $2 trillion.

The book *War Finance* describes three ways to pay for armed conflict. The first involves going into debt. A country decides to worry about paying for the war after it is over and borrows money to pay for the extra expenses. The second method is taxation—the government requires that people pay more taxes and spends the extra money on the military. A third method is seigniorage. It is the profit a government can make between the actual cost of making a coin and its face value. If it costs the government 10 cents to make a quarter, but consumers value it at 25 cents, the government makes 15 cents on every coin.

The U.S. Civil War (1861–64) presents an illuminating look at war finance. The northern states raised money through borrowing and taxation. Congress raised existing taxes or instituted new taxes on all sorts of products. In 1861, the United States also introduced its first income tax. The South tried to borrow money to pay for war costs. When it could not borrow enough money, the Confederacy turned to its printing presses, simply producing paper money to pay its bills. Unfortunately, such money is subject to *inflation,* a decrease in the money's purchasing power as prices continually rise. By the war's end, Confederate money had suffered a 9,000 percent loss in purchasing power.

ENVIRONMENTAL COSTS

An article appearing in 2000 in the *Canadian Medical Association Journal* discussed the effects of war on health and the environment. The author suggested that military actions may exert four long-term effects on societies worldwide.

First, nuclear weapons have the capacity to destroy civilization and perhaps life on earth. Even if those weapons are never used, making and testing them creates **radioactive** waste that endangers living things, including humans.

The second area of concern comes from conventional bombing. Bombing destroys the infrastructure of a city—the built-in systems that allow people to live, work, and travel among other things.

The third area of concern focuses on the effects of land mines. The International Committee for the Red Cross estimates that between 100 and 120 million of these have been buried in nations around the world over the last 60 years. Many of these relics from old wars are still active. The Federation of American Scientists Web site estimates that 26,000 people a year—500 a week—are killed or wounded by land mines. Land mines may be set off by farming or by children playing in an open field.

Finally, many military organizations intentionally destroy plant life and trees in war zones. Doing so diminishes the enemy's ability to secure food and deprives enemy soldiers of places to hide. The practice can also cause famine and starvation among the civilian population and often takes years to reverse.

COSTS TO THE FAMILY AND SOCIAL STRUCTURE

War also has an impact on civilians, including young children. Magne Raundalen, an internationally respected psychologist who specializes in treating children damaged by war or terror, was interviewed on Australian radio about the effects of the latest fighting on Iraqi children.

Raundalen maintained that these young people have three concerns about living in a war zone. They might be killed. They might be left alone after losing other members of their family. Finally, they are fearful about the future—what will be left for them after the war is over. Exposure to the ugliness of war leaves most children with emotional health issues that are likely to last a lifetime. Some have to deal with anxiety disorders—persistent, disturbing fears and possible flashbacks to terrifying wartime moments.

Since the mid-1990s, Dutch researchers have studied the impact of war on the ability of civilians to trust and have positive social relationships. Work with civilians who survived World War II showed that memories of wartime incidents remained years after the war ended, affecting sleep patterns and making it hard for some people to be optimistic about the future. Witnessing wartime violence and living through it destroys trust and optimism. Victims often lack a sense of security.

COSTS IN HUMAN LIFE

Perhaps the highest cost of war is counted in human lives. According to the U.S. Department of Defense, the Vietnam War took the lives of nearly 60,000 American servicemen and women. Nearly 20 years after the conflict, the Vietnamese government released figures that 1.1 million military people and 4 million civilians died during the war.

Before the 20th century, military planners concentrated on destroying the enemy's armed forces. However, the concept of total war has turned many civilians into targets. The *Encyclopaedia Britannica* estimated casualties for World War I at 8.5 million soldiers. However, 13 million civilians also died in that war. Casualty estimates for World War II ran even higher, with many sources quoting 50 million or more. The statistics quoted by the *Encyclopaedia Britannica* add up to 19,420,000 military deaths on both sides, with an additional 27,420,000 civilians, leaving a casualty total of almost 48 million. If those figures seem frightening, consider this—they do *not* include the vast numbers of people who were wounded, crippled, or blinded by that war.

TERRORIST ACTS

Many conflicts in the 20th century involved acts of terrorism. Terrorists are people who use violence as a weapon—to instill fear, influence political action, and promote a political or religious cause. Their focus is not an opposing army but a civilian population.

Between 1991 and 1995, a three-way struggle between the major ethnic groups in the former country of Yugoslavia took 250,000 lives. Militias formed by some ethnic groups in that struggle used rape and murder to drive other ethnic groups from their homes—an ugly process known as "ethnic cleansing."

In Rwanda, an African nation, terrorist acts by the Hutu tribe resulted in the murders of 800,000 members of the rival group, the Tutsis, within just three months. Many women were raped and mutilated before being murdered. Special efforts were made to eliminate anyone who might testify about the slaughter. In other parts of the world, conflicts may not reach such bloody levels, but the killing goes on for decades.

The use of terrorism allows a small number of people to have a huge impact. Counterterrorism expert Gayle Rivers explains the effect very simply in his book, *The War Against the Terrorists:* "Kill one, frighten a million."

Terrorists seek out civilian targets, not only because it is easier to attack unarmed civilians than soldiers, but also because a well-placed bomb in a shopping mall guarantees publicity for the terrorists and their cause.

Consider the grim mathematics of September 11, 2001. At the cost of the lives of 19 terrorists, Al Qaeda destroyed the World Trade Center and damaged the Pentagon, the military headquarters of the United States. The attacks killed more than 3,000 people and generated weeks of media coverage. On September 10, 2001, few people knew anything about Al Qaeda. After September 11, no one could pick up a newspaper or turn on a television or radio without hearing about the group.

Fact Or Fiction?

Violence never solves anything.

Fact: Looking back at history, one might discover that violence has solved a number of things. For instance, the Revolutionary War determined whether Americans would remain British colonists or become citizens of a nation of their own. The Civil War solved the problem of slavery. World War II removed the Nazis from power, freed countries around the world from dictatorships, and ended Japanese military ambitions. Fifty years of military preparedness and resistance also ended the threat of Communism.

Studies of history also show that solving one problem is no guarantee of living "happily ever after"—new problems keep developing.

THE CHANGING NATURE OF WAR

Wars are changing. Today few wars involve only military targets. Civilians are increasingly involved. Their involvements raises the costs of war immeasurably.

See also: Community and Violence; Weapons of Violence

FURTHER READING

Brownlie, Alison. *Why Do People Fight Wars?* Austin, Tex.: Raintree/ Steck-Vaugh, 2002.

■ WEAPONS OF VIOLENCE

Instruments that can be used for offense or defense in combat. Conventional weapons may fire projectiles, like bullets or cannon balls, or have sharp edges that cut. However, many seemingly harmless objects can be turned into weapons, like baseball bats, pieces of pipe, or even broken glass bottles.

GUNS

Guns have long been a part of American life, from the Kentucky long rifle to the Colt six-shooter. Americans own weapons for many reasons. Some keep a gun in their homes for protection. Others use them for hunting and sport shooting. Still others use guns to intimidate or bully.

Illegal ownership and use of guns fueled a jump in crime from the 1980s through the 1990s. Guns were the weapon most used in assault and robbery, murder, and suicide. The surge in gun-related violence resulted in what some have called an epidemic of youth violence.

Laurence Steinberg, a psychologist specializing in adolescent development, observed, "What is different about youth violence in America is not that the violence our young people commit is more frequent, but that it is more lethal, and this is because of the weapons they use."

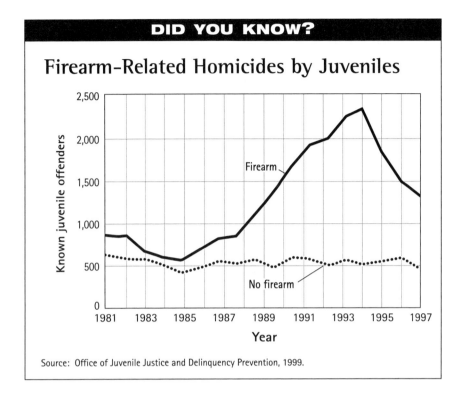

DID YOU KNOW?

Firearm-Related Homicides by Juveniles

Source: Office of Juvenile Justice and Delinquency Prevention, 1999.

Young people in the United States have access to guns at an earlier and earlier age. The Centers for Disease Control and Prevention (CDC) conduct an assessment of adolescents every two years. The CDC's Youth Risk Behavior Surveillance System (YRBSS) asks several violence-related questions. In the 2003 survey, the CDC learned that about 6.1 percent of all students had carried a gun on at least one of the 30 days preceding the survey. According to the National Center for Injury Prevention and Control, homicide ranks as the second-leading killer of 15- to 24-year-olds and the third-leading killer for the 10–14 and 24–35 age groups. The majority of these homicides are from gun injuries. A 1996 study in the *American Journal of Public Health* indicated that over 20 percent of junior high students carried weapons. According to a 2001 study by the Josephson Institute of Ethics, almost 50 percent of students said they could get a gun if they wanted one.

Guns figure in a majority of crimes committed in the United States. According to the 2003 Bureau of Justice Statistics report, guns were used in 67 percent of all murders, 42 percent of all robberies, and 18 percent of all assaults, plus 57 percent of suicides. Firearms were used in 10,159 murders, while the use of other weapons combined totaled just over 5,000. Over 350,000 victims of violent crime (rape and sexual assault, robbery, aggravated assault) faced a gun during the crime.

PHYSICAL FIGHTS

Fists, feet, and nails can also be used as weapons. High school students reported in the 2001 YRBSS that 33 percent had been in a physical fight during the previous year. Over 40 percent of the boys and 25 percent of girls reported fighting in the previous year at least one time. More than 4 percent of these students were hurt badly enough to seek medical attention after the fight.

A number of schools have set out to teach students that violence is not the only response to conflict. Violence prevention programs include the development of skills in anger management, conflict resolution, problem solving, and stress management. When students possess these skills, they are more likely to avoid violence.

CUTTING OBJECTS

Knives and other sharp objects can also serve as weapons. According to the Bureau of Justice Statistics, knives and other sharp objects played a part in 6.4 percent of all violent crime in 2002. That year, 5,315,500 violent crimes took place in the United States, which means that knives figured in approximately 340,000 of those crimes. Blade weapons were used in 80,000 robberies, 250,000 aggravated assaults (assaults where the attacker used a weapon), and 10,000 rapes or sexual assaults.

Many people who might find it difficult to get a gun can easily buy a knife. Box cutters, for instance, are used in most stores to unpack merchandise. The cutter retracts into the handle, so it's convenient. One can carry it in a pocket. The tool is inexpensive and readily available. Some cities have tried to ban the sale of box cutters to people under the age of 18. A 1999 New York City press release described an undercover sting operation in which teens went into stores to buy box cutters. Of the 52 shops tested, 25 percent sold this potential weapon.

Two years later, terrorist hijackers carried box cutters on at least one of the planes used in the attacks on September 11, 2001.

FIRES AND BOMBS

Arson is a crime; it is the intentional, malicious burning of a building. The National Fire Protection Association (NFPA) reported 418,000 intentional fires in 1999. Those fires were responsible for 622 deaths and caused $2.7 billion in damages. Law enforcement officials have a difficult time finding those responsible for arson. In 1999, only 16 percent of all arsons resulted in an arrest. Almost half of those arrested were under the age of 18. In fact, the NFPA says that juveniles make up the highest percentage of arsonists. Over half of all arson crimes are committed by youths under the age 18, with one-third under the age of 15, and 5 percent under the age of 10.

Fire also results from the use of bombs, especially in a military situation. By the end of 2003, some 35 military conflicts around the world provided ample opportunity for the use of explosives, whether fired from artillery pieces or dropped from airplanes.

Advancements in technology have considerably improved airplane bombing runs. So-called **smart bombs** incorporate video cameras and guidance systems. Using information relayed back to the bomber, personnel aboard the airplane can direct the bomb's course, much as people control movement on a video game screen.

Fact Or Fiction?

If some country starts making nukes, we ought to go in there and stop them.

Fact: Some countries have moved to stop others from trying to develop nuclear weapons, usually by intercepting scientific equipment before it reaches the nuclear researchers. In 1981, Israeli warplanes attacked and destroyed the Osirak nuclear facility in Iraq, destroying it. At the time, Iraq was believed to be within years of creating a nuclear bomb.

Unfortunately, it is often difficult to tell exactly how far a nation has come along the road to nuclear capability. In 1998, India detonated three nuclear bombs, surprising the world and U.S. intelligence agencies. Even through the country was under the surveillance of spy satellites, intelligence analysts did not detect the preparations for the underground tests.

As one of the Indian nuclear researchers put it in a 1998 *National Review* article, "It's a matter on their intelligence being good, our deception being better."

The most powerful weapon today is the nuclear bomb. Only a few countries have developed nuclear capability, but the fact that a number of nations are trying to build these weapons is of grave concern to military and political leaders worldwide. Nuclear bombs achieve their destructive power by forcing atoms to split, releasing tremendous amounts of energy. From the 1950s through the 1980s, the cold war—the political and military conflict between the United States and the former Soviet Union—spurred the creation of huge nuclear arsenals. Many people believed the world would soon be destroyed. The missiles were never used. Today, many fear that the technology for creating those nuclear weapons will fall into the hands of terrorists.

Nuclear bombs saw combat action only at the end of World War II. In 1944, the United States became the only nation to ever use nuclear weapons in combat. The nation dropped two atom bombs on Japan: one on Hiroshima and one on Nagasaki. The toll was devastating. Over 200,000 people were killed. When a nuclear bomb explodes, it immediately creates an intense, incomparable surge of heat that reaches 300 million degrees centigrade at its core. When these bombs were dropped, the top of the cloud formed by the blast reached 17,000 feet. Everyone within 1,000 yards of the blast died, and people as far away as two miles needed significant medical attention for radiation burns. Buildings were immediately consumed in the blast. In total, the first atom bomb killed between 30 and 40 percent of the population of Hiroshima.

The tragedy does not end there, however. A nuclear explosion produces more than heat. It creates debris that radiates nuclear particles and energy waves. These **radioactive** by-products are extremely harmful to living things. Radioactive fallout stays in the air and collects on the ground, causing many health problems for people in the area. In the months after the Hiroshima bombing, residents developed massive scar tissue from burns, cataracts, leukemia and other cancers, hair loss, birth defects, and infertility. It may be another hundred years before we know the true long-term consequences.

CHEMICAL AND BIOLOGICAL WEAPONS

Chemical weapons are devices designed to cause death or other harm through the poisonous properties of chemicals. **Biological weapons** use disease-causing organisms like bacteria or viruses, or toxins (poisons) found in nature to kill or incapacitate people. Along with nuclear weapons, these devices are called **weapons of mass destruction** because of the dangers they pose. These weapons can destroy the lives of thousands, even millions of people.

Chemical warfare was introduced during World War I with the use of poison gas. More recently these weapons have been associated with terrorists. In 1995, Japanese cult members released sarin in the Tokyo subway. Sarin is a **nerve gas,** a chemical agent that attacks the human nervous system. The poison gas was released in several places in the subway system, killing 11 and injuring 5,500 people.

In 2001, during the weeks after September 11, letters containing spores of anthrax, a deadly disease, were sent to five media offices and two U.S. senators. As a result of their exposure to the disease, 22 people were infected with anthrax, and five died of inhalation anthrax. Two of the fatalities occurred after anthrax powder contaminated the mail as it was being processed at a postal facility.

During the dictatorship of Saddam Hussein, Iraq developed an arsenal of chemical weapons that were used during the Iran-Iraq War and to put down internal rebellions. Concern that Iraq was developing new and more dangerous weapons of mass destruction was a major rationale for the American-led invasion that deposed Saddam Hussein.

Weapons were probably among the earliest tools developed by humankind. Science and technology have allowed the production of increasingly sophisticated weapons. One fact remains, however. Whether it is a complicated virus developed in a laboratory or an improvised club snatched up from the street, weapons can—and often do—kill.

See also: Criminals and Violent Activity; Drugs and Violence; Teens and Violence; War

FURTHER READING
Guy, John. *Weapons and Warfare.* New York: Barrons, 1998.

■ WORKPLACE VIOLENCE

A variety of aggressive and harmful behaviors that take place in factories, offices, and other places of business. At times, workplace violence has featured prominently in the news, as the following stories suggest. In August 2003, a former employee, fired six months earlier, returned to a Chicago plant with firearms and killed six former coworkers. In July 2003, an Alabama Lockheed Martin employee left a mandatory training session and returned with a rifle, murdering five fellow employees. In September 2002, an insurance executive in New York City shot two coworkers in his office and then killed himself.

Although stories like these are almost guaranteed a splashy headline, they only represent a small part of workplace violence. A 1999 report for the U.S. Department of Justice estimated that nearly 2 million incidents of workplace violence occur every year. They result in about $36 billion in lost production, lost time, legal fees, and payments to injured workers.

When the media discusses workplace violence, it usually concentrates on murder and **sexual harassment**—unwelcome sexual advances, requests for sexual favors, or other verbal or physical conduct of a sex-

---

DID YOU KNOW?

Occupations with Highest Rates of Workplace Homicides

Occupation	Number of homicides per 100,000 employees per year
Store owners and managers	1065
Law enforcement officers	520
Taxicab drivers/chauffeurs	289
Stock handlers/baggers	260
Security guards	253
Gas station workers	164
Bartenders	84
Hotel clerks	40

Source: National Institute for Occupational Safety and Health, 1995.

ual nature that are made conditions of employment, used as a basis for employment decisions or create a work environment that interferes with job performance. Less newsworthy but still dangerous situations include threats from angry customers and patrons, worker/management disputes, and abusive initiation rites for new employees.

Regardless of the type of violence people encounter at work, common threads connect these incidents. A 1996 article in the *Journal of Occupational and Environmental Medicine* discussed common factors related to workplace violence. Work environments with high levels of stress can lead to violence. When plants close or companies engage in downsizing, reducing the number of employees, violence may also result. Workplaces that condone on-the-job bullying may foster confrontations when those who have been bullied become so stressed that they resort to violence. People with jobs in health care, social services, and other industries that deal directly with the public may also encounter violence in the workplace.

HAZING IN THE WORKPLACE

Hazing is a form of initiation. New members of an organization are required to perform humiliating tasks or face rough practical jokes as a condition of employment. Sometimes workplace hazing is just silly, like having "the new kid" look for forms that don't exist or asking a new worker to pick up a tool that has been welded to the floor. However, these rites can isolate new workers, with veterans treating them like second-class citizens, verbally harassing them, and even interfering with their work.

The employee-rights organization Job Watch reports that hazing activities often escalate. The longer rituals are allowed to continue, the more extreme they can become. Some workers simply can't handle the abuse physically or emotionally. Employees may become depressed, experience a lack of desire to return to work, or be generally unproductive at work. Some people have more extreme reactions, resulting in shooting incidents much like the ones in high schools where victims of bullying lash out at those abusing them.

UNIONS AND ANGER

In many industries, workers have joined labor unions to protect their rights, improve working conditions, and seek higher compensation. When negotiations between labor and management fail to resolve a conflict, the union may call a **strike,** or work stoppage. The United

States has a more violent history of labor relations compared to many other industrial nations. As the book *The War on Labor and the Left* points out, 700 American strikers were killed in labor disputes between 1877 and 1968. In Britain, only one striker has been killed since 1911.

Strikes are often emotional times, with feelings running high between those who have walked off the job and those who refuse to honor picket lines. Even old friends can find themselves on opposite sides. Since President Ronald Reagan replaced nearly all of the country's air traffic controllers after a strike in the 1980s, more and more employers have chosen to bring in what they call "replacement workers" when unions attempt to shut down workplaces. Union members see these workers as "strikebreakers" and "scabs."

The use of replacement workers has resulted in longer strikes, greater hardship for strikers, anger, and violence. The National Institute for Labor Relations Research, a pro-management organization, identified 8,799 incidents of labor union violence in the news between 1975 and 1998. The organization has also complained of a "loophole" created by the U.S. Supreme Court in laws to control labor unions. When striking electricians were accused of sabotaging company equipment, the Court ruled that the action was fair, because workers were trying to advance their union's legitimate objectives.

Based on this decision, only 258 convictions have resulted from the 8,799 accusations over the past 23 years. Replacement workers and those who chose not to participate in strikes have faced verbal threats and harassment, physical attacks, and even murder.

RESPONSES TO HARASSMENT

Sexual harassment has become a growing problem over the last 60 years, as more and more women have entered the workforce. Harassment includes unwanted touching or grabbing, sexual advances, requests for sexual favors, sexual jokes, or constant pestering for a date. Turning down these advances often has a negative impact on a person's chances for promotion or pay increases.

Q & A

Question: If I meet someone I like at work, do sexual harassment laws prohibit me from asking him/her out on a date?

Answer: Technically, no, although for many reasons it is not advised you date a coworker. Harassment has to do with the creation of a threatening, intimidating, or hostile work environment. If you ask, and the person says no, then you have to let it go. If you keep asking, then you cross a line. If turning you down means that the individual will be punished in some way at work, then you have also crossed the line.

In formerly all-male work environments, crude jokes, offensive language, macho horseplay, and posting pinups or centerfolds were tolerated and even accepted. These behaviors and many others are not appropriate in mixed company. By the 1960s, those behaviors were not only offensive, but also illegal. Lawsuits based on Title VII of the Civil Rights Act of 1964 forced many companies to make changes in the workplace.

Through the 1980s and 1990s, many companies began to establish rules of behavior. The penalties for violating these rules often began with a warning but could lead to dismissal if the behavior and the attitudes that prompted that behavior did not change. The law emphasized the dangers of creating "a hostile work environment."

One of the best ways to prevent harassment is to improve one's communication skills. Men and women are socialized differently in the United States, making it easy for someone to say or do the wrong thing at the wrong time. If someone has said something that offends a coworker, immediate communication can minimize the damage. The person who is offended should explain why the remark or action was distasteful, and the offender should apologize.

Fact Or Fiction?

Workplace shootings are the most common form of workplace violence.

Fact: Murder at work makes up a very small percentage of workplace violence. In fact, only one out of every 2,000 acts of workplace violence results in death. It seems high because the murders are the only part of workplace violence the media covers. Almost 400,000 aggravated assaults (assaults with a weapon) occur each year at work, most of those as a carryover from domestic violence incidents. More than half of all violent incidents are threats of physical harm, harassment, or other acts which create an unhealthy environment to work in.

WORKPLACE VIOLENCE PREVENTION

In response to the problems associated with workplace violence, many organizations and consultants have developed programs to protect employees. A 1996 joint project by the Occupational Safety and Health Administration and the Long Island Coalition for Workplace Violence Awareness and Prevention outlined the elements of a workplace violence prevention program. It begins with a company putting its policies in writing and making them available to all employees. Every employee–including supervisors–should be trained in putting these policies into action.

Organized teams examine the company's business facilities to assess the vulnerability of employees to four kinds of violence–from strangers, clients or customers, coworkers, and personal relationships. A workplace violence program must also address security issues. Do people work alone? Are they responsible for valuable items? Are staffing levels appropriate? Do workers have training to anticipate problems and control them? Does the company's written violence prevention policies treat all employees fairly? Have they been trained to resolve conflicts and disputes? Does the program allow employees to restrict access by family members? Do supervisors have training to deal with family violence issues and keep the situation confidential?

The U.S. Office of Personnel Management also maintains information on workplace violence prevention. These are indicators that may help to identify potentially dangerous workers:

- Direct or veiled threats of harm
- Intimidating, belligerent, harassing, bullying, or other inappropriate and aggressive behavior
- Numerous conflicts with supervisors and other employees
- Bringing a weapon to the workplace, brandishing a weapon in the workplace, making inappropriate references to guns, or showing a fascination with weapons
- Statements showing fascination with incidents of workplace violence, statements indicating approval of the use of violence to resolve a problem, or statements indicating identification with perpetrators of workplace homicides

- Statements indicating desperation (over family, financial, and other personal problems) to the point of contemplating suicide
- Drug/alcohol abuse
- Extreme changes in behaviors.

While the guidelines warn that participants in the program must avoid **profiling**—judging individuals by stereotypes—the behaviors listed cannot be ignored.

Americans work hard. Worrying about harassment or violence at work makes a tough job even tougher. Awareness of the kinds of problems one can face plus proper training to deal with them can go a long way toward avoiding workplace violence.

See also: Assault and Bullying; School Violence; Sexual Violence

FURTHER READING

Chaiet, Donna. *Staying Safe at Work.* New York: Rosen Publishing Group, 1995.

HOTLINES
AND HELP SITES

D.A.R.E. (Drug Abuse Resistance Education) America
URL: http://www.dare.com
Phone: 1-800-223-DARE (3273)
Mission: Founded in 1983 in Los Angeles, D.A.R.E. has proven so successful that it is now being implemented in nearly 80 percent of our nation's school districts and in more than 54 countries around the world. This year 36 million school children around the world—26 million in the United States—will benefit from D.A.R.E., which gives kids the skills they need to avoid involvement in drugs, gangs, and violence.
Programs: A police officer–led series of classroom lessons that teaches children from kindergarten through 12th grade how to resist peer pressure and live productive drug- and violence-free lives

Division of Violence Prevention,
   National Center for Injury Prevention and Control (NCIPC),
   Centers for Disease Control and Prevention (CDC)
URL: http://www.cdc.gov/ncipc
Phone: 770-488-4362
Mission: The CDC provides credible information to enhance health decisions and promotes health through strong partnerships. The NCIPC focuses on helping people avoid injuries, both unintentional and intentional.
Programs: The Division of Violence Prevention has represented the CDC's focus on violence prevention since the early 1980s, when

efforts included the prevention of youth violence, suicide, and suicide attempts. The division offers information in the areas of child
maltreatment, intimate partner violence, sexual violence, suicide,
and youth violence.

G.R.E.A.T. (Gang Resistance Education and Training)
URL: http://www.great-online.org
Phone: 1-800-726-7070
Mission: Designed to help children set goals for themselves, resist
pressures, learn how to resolve conflicts without violence, and
understand how gangs and youth violence impact the quality of
their lives
Programs: A school-based program developed by the Bureau of
Alcohol, Tobacco, Firearms, and Explosives and other federal law
enforcement agencies. G.R.E.A.T. students discover for themselves
the ramifications of gang and youth violence through structured
exercises and interactive approaches to learning. The program provides training and a classroom curriculum.

National Center for Victims of Crime
URL: http://www.ncvc.org
Phone: 202-467-8700
National helpline: 1-800-FYI-CALL (394-2255)
Mission: To forge a national commitment to help victims of crime
rebuild their lives. Dedicated to serving individuals, families, and
communities harmed by crime
Programs: Since 1985, the organization has worked with more than
10,000 grassroots organizations and criminal justice agencies serving millions of crime victims. It offers supportive counseling, practical information about crime and victimization, referrals to local
community resources, as well as skilled advocacy in the criminal
justice and social service systems.

National Domestic Violence Hotline
URL: http://www.ndvh.org
Phone: 1-800-799-SAFE (7233)
Mission: To answer phone calls from victims of domestic violence, fam-
ily members, and friends from all over the world for crisis interven-
tion, referrals, and general information about domestic violence

Programs: With a database of more than 4,000 shelters and service providers across the United States, Puerto Rico, Alaska, Hawaii, and the U.S. Virgin Islands, the hotline provides callers with information they might otherwise have found difficult or impossible to obtain. The hotline is available 24 hours a day, 365 days a year.

National Hopeline Network: Kristin Brooks Hope Center
URL: http://www.hopeline.com
Phone: 540-338-5756
Hotline: 1-800-SUICIDE (784-2433)
Mission: A nonprofit organization dedicated to suicide prevention, intervention, and healing, by providing a single point of entry to community-based crisis services through telephone and Internet-based technologies; by bringing national attention and access to services for postpartum depression and other women's mood disorders; through education and advocacy; through formal research and evaluation of crisis line services; and by championing the need for national funding for community-based suicide prevention crisis services.
Programs: Connects callers to a certified crisis center nearest the caller's location; services are available 24 hours a day, seven days a week.

National Institute on Alcohol Abuse and Alcoholism (NIAAA)
URL: http://www.niaaa.nih.gov
Mission: Provides leadership in the national effort to reduce alcohol-related problems
Programs: Conducts and supports research in a wide range of scientific areas, including genetics, neuroscience, epidemiology, health risks and benefits of alcohol consumption, prevention, and treatment; translates and disseminates research findings to health-care providers, researchers, policy makers, and the public

National Institute on Drug Abuse (NIDA)
URL: http://www.nida.nih.gov
Mission: To lead the nation in bringing the power of science to bear on drug abuse and addiction

Programs: Furthers understanding of how drugs of abuse affect the brain and behavior and ensures the rapid and effective transfer of scientific data to policy makers, drug abuse practitioners, other health-care practitioners, and the general public

National Institute on Media and the Family
Phone: 1-888-672-5437
URL: http://www.mediafamily.org
Mission: Founded by David Walsh, Ph.D., in 1996, this organization examines the impact of electronic media on families, working to help parents and communities monitor what their kids watch
Programs: Provides information about the impact of media on children and gives people who care about children the resources they need to make informed choices

Rape, Abuse & Incest National Network (RAINN)
URL: http://www.rainn.org
Hotline: 1-800-656-HOPE (4673)
Mission: To serve as the nation's largest anti–sexual assault organization
Programs: Offers counseling resources, prevention tips, and news; operates the National Sexual Assault Hotline; and carries out programs to prevent sexual assault, help victims, and ensure that rapists are brought to justice

GLOSSARY

abandonment   to leave or desert a person, especially a person who cannot survive without help

addiction   the state of becoming physically or psychologically dependent on a drug

aggravated assault   a legal term referring to an attack made on a person, usually with a weapon, with the intention of causing serious harm

autonomic nervous system   the part of the nervous system which controls involuntary body actions, such as the beating of the heart

autonomy-oriented   a psychological classification under self-determination theory, describing those who believe their responses and actions come from within themselves

behavior modification   a form of psychological treatment aimed at changing or stopping a destructive or unwanted behavior

Benzedrine   a trademarked name for an amphetamine drug, which acts as a stimulant, speeding up the nervous system and body functions

biological weapons   weapons using disease-causing organisms or poisonous by-products from these organisms to destroy life

cannabis *See* marijuana.

castration the process of removing or depriving the use of the sexual organs

chemical weapons weapons using the poisonous effects of chemical compounds to incapacitate or kill people

chronic community violence a situation where residents in a locality experience frequent and prolonged exposure to weapons, crime, and random acts of violence

cocaine an addictive stimulant drug that speeds up the nervous system and body functions

cognitive behavioral treatment psychological therapy where patients work to understand the thoughts and emotions behind their behavior

community policing policy initiatives to create a partnership between police and communities in preventing crime

community service an alternative to a prison sentence whereby convicted criminal offenders undertake some effort to help the district or locality where they live

conflict resolution the settlement of personal differences between people by means of effective communication, often guided by a mediator

control-oriented a psychological classification under self-determination theory, describing those who believe their behavior is the result of external actions and influences

court costs the expenses involved in administering a legal trial

crack a very powerful, inexpensive form of cocaine

criminal homicide the unlawful taking of a human life, including murder and manslaughter

cycle of events in cognitive-behavioral psychological therapy, the chain of thoughts and incidents that leads up to an action

depressant a drug which depresses, or slows down, the nervous system and body functions

depression a psychological state distinguished by feelings of sadness, low self-worth, and a lack of energy

discipline punishment, especially that which aims to produce improved moral behavior

drive-by shooting a form of intergang violence where groups of gang members in the street are fired upon by rival gang members in a passing car

drug rehabilitation the process by which an addict overcomes dependency on a drug

elder abuse violence expressed against a person 60 years or older, including physical, sexual, and emotional abuse, financial exploitation, abandonment, and neglect

eldercide the murder of an older person, age 65 or older

emotional abuse mistreatment by attacking a person's feelings through threats, humiliation, or other harmful actions

excusable homicide a legal situation where a death occurs as a result of a person's actions but without criminal intent

family breakdown a failing in the family structure where family members no longer feel an emotional connection

felonious homicide *See* criminal homicide.

felony a classification of more serious crimes, punishable by harsher sentences

fighting words forms of expression calculated to inflame listeners and incite violent actions

financial exploitation misusing money or financial resources of persons one is supposed to be caring for

fundamentalism rigid religious belief in a set of principles or an inspired religious text

gatekeeper in suicide prevention programs, a person trained to recognize the warning signs of suicide in individuals and who picks such people out of groups, referring them for help

gene a structure that transmits characteristics and functions between generations of living things

genocide the systematic, planned extermination of a racial or cultural group

group therapy a form of psychological treatment involving interaction between more than one patient

guided self-help program a form of self-improvement undertaken with information and advice from a therapist, book, computer program, or the like

hallucinogen a drug which causes false perceptions of reality for users

hardy personality a psychological classification of people who can successfully handle stress

hazing a form of initiation for new members of a group, usually involving the accomplishment of difficult or humiliating tasks or undergoing practical jokes

hormone a body chemical which affects various organs, initiating, stopping, or modifying its function

individual self-help a form of dealing with problems by working on them alone and by helping others, as occurs in recovery groups like Alcoholics Anonymous

infanticide taking the life of a child less than five years old

inhalants intoxicating substances which cause dizziness and other effects by being breathed in, such as aerosol fumes

intimate partner abuse acts of verbal or physical violence against a spouse, a live-in lover, or between people who are dating

intravenous into or involving the veins, as in the term intravenous drug abuse, where substances are injected into the body through the veins

juvenile court a legal system devised to deal with criminal behavior by young people, with the aim of helping them develop into useful members of society

laws the body of rules governing the affairs of a community, state, or nation

mandatory sentencing laws legal articles setting forth strict guidelines for federal judges in sentencing convicted offenders

manslaughter the taking of human life without the intention of doing injury

marijuana an intoxicating plant which, when smoked, causes feelings of euphoria—great happiness—in users

methamphetamines an addictive stimulant drug that speeds up the nervous system and body functions

misdemeanor a legal classification of less serious crimes, punished with a fine or a brief prison sentence

murder the intentional taking of a human life

narcotics drugs that dull the senses, bring on sleep, and, with continued use, result in addiction

negative reinforcement   a psychological term for a punishment or unwelcome result coming from a particular behavior

neglect   failure to provide for a child's or adult's basic needs; can be emotional, psychological, or physical

nerve gas   a chemical weapon which attacks the function of the nerves, thereby paralyzing the muscles they control

neurotransmitters   body chemicals which transmit information from one nerve cell to another

overdose   taking an excessive or fatal dose of a drug

parole   the release of a prisoner before his or her sentence is over, on the condition of the person's good behavior

peer mediation   a method of resolving conflicts where both of the arguing sides work with an equal in their community to develop a compromise

physical abuse   inflicting pain or physical harm on a person

positive reinforcement   a psychological term for a reward of desired result coming from a particular behavior

prejudice   a judgment about people or things formed in advance, without examining the facts

probation   the action of suspending a legal sentence and granting freedom to a convicted offender on the promise of good behavior

profiling   the process of developing a list of characteristics about a particular offender; also using lists of characteristics indiscriminately to identify whole classes of people as potential offenders

rape   sexual intercourse achieved against another person's will by force or the threat of force

recidivism a tendency to fall back into former behavior, especially criminal habits

relapse prevention a form of psychological therapy aimed at keeping people from falling back into unwelcome forms of behavior

robbery unlawfully taking the property of another through force or threat of force

sedative a drug with a calming, tranquilizing effect

self-determination theory a psychological theory that views people's motives and personalities as expressions of free will

serotonin a body chemical found mainly in the brain that is capable of raising body temperature, controlling certain types of muscles, and changing behavior

sexual abuse forcing or tricking another person into unwanted sexual contact

sexual bribery using a superior social or employment position to offer desirable consideration in return for sexual favors

sexual coercion using a superior social or employment position to threaten a person into offering sexual favors

skinheads followers of extreme political movements advocating racial superiority, so named because of the extremely short haircuts they favor

smart bomb explosive weapons that can be dropped from airplanes and guided to targets

stereotype an oversimplified and often inaccurate idea, opinion, or belief

steroid or 'roid rage outbursts of anger caused by body chemistry imbalances due to the use of steroid drugs

stimulant a drug which speeds up the nervous system and body functions

stressor anything that causes stress

strike a work stoppage by employees, especially employees organized in a union

terrorism the use of violence and fear to achieve an end, especially a political end

three Cs of hardiness commitment, challenge, and control; elements in creating a personality that will resist stress

token economy an element of behavior modification that offers rewards for desired behavior

tolerance the process by which a human body becomes accustomed to an addictive substance, requiring larger and larger doses to achieve a high

trigger a psychological term for an event which stimulates anger and may provoke a violent response

truth-in-sentencing laws legal controls ensuring that imprisoned offenders serve at least 85 percent of their sentences

turf territory controlled by a gang

weapons of mass destruction certain forms of arms—nuclear, biological, or chemical weapons—that can cause widespread damage either to property or to populations

withdrawal the physical symptoms connected with ending the use of addictive drugs

INDEX

Boldface page numbers indicate major treatment of a topic; *italics* indicate illustrations.

A

abuse, child. *See* child abuse; family violence
acquaintance rape 98–99
Administration for Children and Families 37–38
aggravated assault, defined 3, 26
alcohol and violence 13–17. *See also* criminals and violent activity; media and violence; school violence; teens and violence; violent behavior, causes of
    cultural expectations and alcohol 16
    effect of alcohol on body 13–14
    fact vs. fiction 14
    perpetrators of violence and 7
    personality and 15–16
    questions and answers 15
    readings 17
    theories on link between 14–15
Alcoholics Anonymous 106
Alice in Chains 33
Al Qaeda 133
American Academy of Pediatrics (APA) 38
American Journal of Community Psychology 100
American Journal of Psychiatry 123–134
American Journal of Public Health 135
American Journal of Sociology 75
American Medical Association 37
American Prosecutors Resource Center 117
American Psychological Association (APA)
    communities and violence 24
    family violence 42
    fight or flight response 44
    homicide 63
    self-mutilation 93
American Psychologist 22, 23
American Street Gang, The (Klein) 51, 54
anthrax 139
Anti-Defamation League 60
antisocial behavior 118
APA. *See* American Psychological Association (APA)
assault and bullying 17–21, 115. *See also* criminals and violent activity; media and violence; school violence; teens and violence; violent behavior, causes of
    aggravated assault 3, 26

bullying, generally 1, 6, 16
    dealing with bullying 21
    defined 3
    description of bullying 16
    effects of bullying 19–20
    fact vs. fiction 18–19, 115–116
    female bullying 18–19, 20–21
    percentage of students bullied at school, by grade *19*
    readings 21
    simple assault 4
    teens speak 20–21
    victims of 115–117
    workplace 141
Australian Institute of Criminology 78
autonomic nervous system (ANS) 43–44
avoidance, as mood enhancement method 47

B

Behavioral Science and the Law 78
behavior modification 78
biological influences, violent behavior 125–128
biological weapons 139
Blackboard Jungle, The (film) 49
Black's Law Dictionary 61
Blind Melon 33
Block Watch 70
Bloods (gang) 49
bombs 137–138
Boy Scouts 70
British Association of Social Workers 102
British Journal of Psychology 112
British Parliament
    sexual violence hotline 101
Building Coalitions 101 24
Bureau of Alcohol, Tobacco, and Firearms 69
Bureau of Justice Statistics
    Cost of Violent Crime, The 103, 104
    Crime Victimization 103
    criminals and violent activity 27
    family violence 37
    homicide 62
    parole 79
    rape 97